Bon Appetit, Giovanna

Entirely Entertaining
IN THE
Bonnet House
Style

Bonnet House and Gardens
Fort Lauderdale, Florida

Bonnet House Mission Statement

The Mission of Bonnet House, Inc. is to document, preserve, and interpret the winter estate of Frederic and Evelyn Bartlett to reflect their lifestyle, interests and highly personal aesthetic sense.

The vision: Bonnet House will be a nationally recognized historic museum and gardens that inspires in its diverse audience a delight in creative expression; an appreciation of the property's history, art, decorative arts, architecture, gardens and ecology; and an understanding of the importance of historic preservation.

Entirely Entertaining
IN THE Bonnet House Style

Copyright © 2001
Bonnet House Alliance
900 N. Birch Road
Fort Lauderdale, Florida 33304
Phone: 954-563-5393
Fax: 954-561-4174
www.bonnethouse.com

Library of Congress Number: 2001   130642
ISBN: 0-9624757-4-2

Designed, Edited, and Manufactured by
Favorite Recipes® Press
An imprint of

FRP

P.O. Box 305142
Nashville, Tennessee 37230
1-800-358-0560

Designer: Starletta Polster
Art Director: Steve Newman
Project Manager: Susan Larson

Manufactured in the United States of America
First Printing: 2001   5,000 copies

Table of Contents

Sponsors

We gratefully acknowledge the financial assistance of the following corporations and individual friends of Bonnet House. Their contributions exemplify their support of the mission of Bonnet House to document, preserve, and interpret this valuable property.

Grand Patron

Northern Trust Bank

Patrons

AutoNation	Gill Hotels
Bonnet House Alliance	Kitchens to Go
Cookbook Steering Committee	Publix Super Market Charities
Devereaux Bruch	*Sun-Sentinel*

Sponsors

A Bonnet House Friend	Elizabeth Buntrock

Swan Category

Shirley Beal	Jan Handley
Bonnet House Staff	Lago Mar Properties
Patty & Ed Buchser	Doretta Penn
Barbara Cooper	Lois Schmatz
Sarah & Tom Flood	

Sponsors

Sponsors

Shell Category

Bonnet House Junior Alliance
Corliss Bennett
Sue & Jim Camp
Sandra Casteel
Georgia & Howard Elfman
Suan Grant
Ann & Bob Gremillion
Irene R. Hart
Le Club International
Private Residences & Marina
Betty Leonard

Susan & Buddy Lochrie
Anne Lombard
Lynne & Ralph McGrath
Sharon & Win Menish
Barbara Middlebrooks
Miller, Schwartz & Miller
Geri & Bryan Murray
Ann Powell
Alice W. Smith
Vivien Sterghos
Meg Stone

Cygnet Category

Marguerite Akin
Kay Anselmo
Joan F. Babson
Jo Bonura
Jane G. Brobst
Betsy Crudele
Barbara Sloan Edelson
Shirley Gleason
Josephine Grelet
Joan Jessiman
Barbara Keith
Glenda Kelly

Vikki Kirby
Elli Leutheuser
Pat Breslin Miller
Janet Molchan
Phyllis A. Rasmussen
Wednesdai Rossi
Roger A. Smith
Mary Spilman
Dorothy D. Weston
Claudia & Birch Willey
Fran Young

5

Cookbook Committee Members

Special thanks to the members of the cookbook committee
for their time and expertise in producing
this book honoring the Bartletts and Bonnet House.

Jeanne Bass	Suan Grant	Barbara Middlebrooks
Shirley Beal	Anne Gremillion	Becky Mussler
Devereaux Bruch	Jan Handley	Sue Nesbit
Patty Buchser	Irene Hart	Doretta Penn
Joanne Carey	Patsy Hawkes	Ann Powell
Sandra Casteel	Susu Johnson	Lois Schmatz
Barbara Cooper	Nancy Kellermeyer	Barbara Schwartz
Denyse Cunningham	Betsy Kornowski	Francine Schwartz
Barbara Sloan Edelson	Joanne Leathe	Suzie Smith
Georgia Elfman	Anne Lombard	Meg Stone
Starr Fisher	Lynne McGrath	Laura Ward

Recipe Contributors and Testers

Entirely Entertaining in the Bonnet House Style is a collection of recipes
selected from over seven hundred submitted. We thank all of those who
shared their recipes and those who tested the recipes. We apologize to
anyone we may have inadvertently failed to mention.

Marguerite Akin	Jeanne Bass	Judy Britton
Judy Allen	Cobey Lou Bastone	Jane G. Brobst
Maria Anderson	Bobbie Baughman	Sally A. Brown
Betty Bakus	Shirley Beal	Devereaux Bruch
Barbara Barber	Corliss Bennett	Petey Buchholz
Carol Bass	Jo Bonura	Patty Buchser

Contributors

Recipe Contributors and Testers

Peter Bundy
Sue Camp
Joanne Carey
Sandra Casteel
Eleanor Cooper
Betsy Crudele
Jean Darling
Jane DePadro
Valentina Distefano
Mitzi Doumar
Sandy Driscoll
Georgia Elfman
Raquel Ferrero
Starr Fisher
Sarah Flood
Connie Folz
Richard French
Kathleen Galvin
Diane Gill
William Goodman
Suan Grant
Kathleen Gray
Jane Greenwasser
Ann Gremillion
Susanne Hamilton
Jan Handley
Irene Hart
Carolyn Hatfield
Barbara Henninger
Joan Hippler
Mitzi Hirt
Carol Howe
Joan Jessiman

Patti Kearson
Barbara Keith
Nancy Kellermeyer
Deborah Kerr
Betsy Kornowski
Marcy Lambert
Joanne Leathe
Daryl Lenz
Betty Leonard
Diane Linder
Irene Lindon
Marie Little
Anne Lombard
Rosa Lukens
Jackie Lyles
Barbara Marentette
Sally Marshall
Nora Martin
Judy Maus
Carol McCarvill
Ann McCrory
Darcy Camp McCurry
Susan McQuillen
Shelley Melvin
Sharon Menish
Barbara Middlebrooks
Pat Breslin Miller
Sheila Moss
Ellen Murton
Becky Mussler
Vera Luci Mustatea
Sue Nesbit
Jack Noble

Betty Osborn
Nancyetta Palumbo
Carol Patten
Doretta Penn
Ann Powell
Carol Powell
Eve Prochaska
Nancy Purdy
Judith Roddewig
Jill and Tracy Rowlett
John Rudra
Lois Schmatz
Francine Schwartz
Daisy Scott
Dottie Shepherd
Shirley Smith
Suzie Smith
Caryl Sorensen
Rae Spellman
Patsy Staletovich
Vivien Sterghos
Nancy Stoll
Mike Stone
Catherine Strong
Carol Teulon
Billie Sue Theoharis
Gini Vyfvinkel
Rosalie Weiss
Jeanette Wenzel
Mary Wilcox
Claudia Willey
Fran C. Young

Evelyn Fortune Bartlett
(1887–1997)

We dedicate this book to Evelyn Bartlett, whose spirit continues to fill Bonnet House long after her death at the age of 109. Although Bonnet House was constructed before Frederic Clay Bartlett brought her to Florida as his bride in 1931, she and Frederic created a simple yet elegant way of life in the 30s and 40s that preceded today's eclectic and relaxed south Florida lifestyle. The many activities carried on at Bonnet House and the preservation of its unique design and tropical environs reflect their happy years here.

Mrs. Bartlett was not only gracious but was also an organized and talented woman who knew how to run a household, foster the work of household staff, and make each meal an artistic masterpiece. She and Frederic enjoyed entertaining friends and relatives for luncheons and dinners, usually at a table set with unique china overlooking the courtyard. On their travels to the islands, they collected seeds to grow the tropical fruits enjoyed as part of their outdoor meals. Some of her paintings of fruits and flowers are part of this cookbook.

Evelyn Bartlett loved animals and birds and kept a small dog as her constant companion. She made friends with the monkeys that lived among the Bonnet House trees and hand-fed them every evening. Exotic birds were accustomed to perching on her shoulder without fear.

Because she wanted to protect the property, her desire was that Bonnet House would be available so that future generations could enjoy this enclave of natural beauty, an example of our long-lost coastal habitat. To this end she gave the property to the general public, and for this she has our praise and gratitude.

"I want it to stay like it was in the old days . . . I don't want it to change."
—Evelyn F. Bartlett

8

*Painting of Evelyn Bartlett with white bird by
Frederic Bartlett, circa 1935.*

About Bonnet House and the Bartletts

Bonnet House was named by Hugh Taylor Birch after the yellow Bonnet Lily that grew in the property's marshland. In the late 1800s, Mr. Birch purchased more than three miles of oceanfront property for less than $1.00 per acre. When his daughter, Helen, married Frederic Bartlett, a widower, in 1919, Mr. Birch gave the couple a "house lot" of about 60 acres with 700 feet along the ocean. The property spanned from the present Intracoastal Waterway to the Atlantic Ocean. Frederic had been inspired by his years of study of the art and architecture in Europe. He was a commissioned muralist in the early 1900s, and several of his works remain today in churches and public buildings in Chicago.

Mr. Bartlett combined his professional experience with his study of European architecture to design a unique house, which would promote a gracious "indoor-outdoor" lifestyle in the tropical setting. Bonnet House became an ongoing creative project for the Bartletts. Frederic continued to add whimsical details such as inlaid shells and coral pieces,

faux marble finishes, and trompe-l'oeil paintings on walls and ceilings. The house included a music room for Helen to pursue her talents and a studio for Frederic.

Helen died of cancer in 1925. As a memorial to her, Frederic gave selected Postimpressionist paintings he and Helen collected during their marriage to The Art Institute of Chicago. In years to come, Mr. Bartlett would donate additional works to this renowned collection, which features master artists such as Gauguin, Matisse, Picasso, Seurat, and Van Gogh. Today, it represents one of the finest private philanthropic gifts of art to an American museum.

Frederic's marriage to Evelyn Fortune Lilly in 1931 began a new era at Bonnet House. It was a marriage of his artistic talent to her keen eye for color, design, and composition. Their talents combined to create a unique, sophisticated lifestyle. In their travels, Evelyn and Frederic collected curios, antiquities, and works of art that were incorporated into the

Frederic Bartlett received his academic art training
from the Royal Academy in Munich.
He then studied in Paris and Munich and was consulted as
an architect as well as commissioned as a muralist.
Bonnet House Archives

property. Seeds from tropical fruits were carefully nurtured on the property. With a birthday gift from her father, Evelyn purchased the Florida Royal Palms that today stand in stately fashion at the edge of the lagoon. To the west, a wetland area of mangrove trees provided a home to manatees, fish, crabs, and shore birds. Evelyn introduced other colorful animals to the property as well. When coffee was served outdoors, monkeys and birds were always a part of the setting.

Entertaining was done against a backdrop of lush vegetation complemented by Frederic's fanciful murals. Evelyn would consult with the chef to select a menu tailored to the tastes of her guests. Linens, silverware, china, and delightful centerpieces were coordinated to match the mood and menu. To accompany the fine fruit grown on the property, fresh foods were flown to Bonnet House from the Bartletts' Essex, Massachusetts, farm, "Bothways." Many meals were served in the courtyard while cranes sampled toasted breads and exotic birds provided a background of song.

After Frederic's death in 1953, Evelyn grew concerned about the future of Bonnet House. Development pushed to the borders of the property. Except for the recreation site Hugh Taylor Birch had willed to the state after his death in 1943, hers became the last piece of undeveloped acreage. To ensure that the property would remain unchanged, she deeded the grounds and home to the Florida Trust for Historic Preservation in 1983. It is listed on the National Register of Historic Places. Evelyn Fortune Bartlett enjoyed her unique home for more than fifty years. Her last visit to Bonnet House was in 1995; she died two years later at 109.

And now: Bonnet House, risen from the dunes in the midst of Fort Lauderdale, sits serenely nestled in splendid trees . . . overlooking its broad, sheltered lagoon, as if floating, preserved in time. This fruitful gift to Florida, an extraordinary asset to the culture and artistic life . . . of the state . . . must live on, a reminder of things past and a precursor for the coming age . . . a unique tribute to Evelyn Bartlett and her wholly memorable husband, Frederic.
— S. Dillon Ripley, The Secretary Emeritus of the Smithsonian Institution

Sponsored by

Sun-Sentinel

Bonnet House East Façade
*The veranda of the house overlooks the lagoon lined with
its signature Florida Royal Palms, providing a peaceful and
serene place to relax at any time of day or evening.*

Tony Branco ©

Tony Branco ©

Tony Branco ©

The large Wedgwood nautilus
shell was used by Evelyn Bartlett
as a centerpiece when fish was
served. She adopted the nautilus
shell as a logo for the estate.

The Bonnet Lily (Nuphar luteum)
is also called Spatterdock
and grows well in the Lily Pond.

The Bonnet House Alliance

The Bonnet House Alliance, organized as a support group in 1986, is integral to the operation of Bonnet House. As volunteers, members conduct tours of the house and property, host events, programs, and workshops, and organize fund-raising events.

Created in celebration of the time-honored tradition of hospitality practiced by Evelyn Bartlett, "Entirely Entertaining" is the Alliance's annual fund-raising luncheon. Her table settings of simple elegance, a reflection of her natural artistic talent, are the inspiration for the theme of the event, which features beautifully set tables for the guests' dining pleasure. Each table design is the creation of a different hostess using her own china, glassware, linens, and decorations. Guests enjoy viewing the tables during a social hour and then are served a lovely meal on the veranda overlooking the lagoon.

Alliance members also support other Bonnet House events through their attendance and volunteer assistance. These include the Young Artists Music Series, featuring evening concerts held outdoors on the veranda lawn under the full moon, and Splendor in the Tropics, a celebration of art and Bonnet House. A juried exhibition of work by local artists is held in the center of the city, and a dinner and auction of the winning art takes place at the house.

Typical educational programs for which the volunteers provide support include classes in art, orchids, wildlife, ecology, and history. Training of volunteers is year-round and intensive, with workshops designed to familiarize them with the history of Bonnet House and its environmental significance.

Memories of Evelyn Bartlett and her strong desire to preserve Bonnet House motivate the Bonnet House Alliance to dedicated and committed volunteer service.

Sponsored by

The Bonnet House Alliance

The Bartlett Lifestyle

When Bonnet House was built as a winter retreat in the early 1920s, Frederic Bartlett designed it to provide a setting for a casual lifestyle, filtered by coastal breezes from the Atlantic Ocean. Situated on thirty-five acres atop a rise of land between the Intracoastal Waterway and the ocean, the house overlooked a spring-fed lagoon. Concrete blocks formed on the site and many native materials were used throughout. Built around a courtyard lushly landscaped with tropical foliage, the house featured a studio for Frederic's painting, a music room, a dining room, a drawing room, a kitchen, and bedrooms. Artistic elements such as ceiling murals and faux painting by Frederic created an air of fantasy. Wooden animal sculptures and carousel animals around the courtyard added a touch of whimsy.

The Bartletts' style of entertaining was what we would today call "casual elegance." Small dinner parties of eight to ten would include houseguests and friends who had driven down from Palm Beach. One Bonnet House guest recalled that being entertained at Bonnet House was like participating in an unfolding drama. Guests were greeted by the butler and escorted to the Shell Museum adjacent to the Orchid House and Bamboo Bar. There they would view the current collection of blooming orchids while sipping their Rangpur Lime Cocktails and enjoying simple hors d'oeuvre. After-dinner entertainment might be viewing home movies in the Island Theater or a musical or dramatic performance on the stage of the Pavilion located at the south end of the property.

Weather permitting, meals would be served at a beautifully appointed table overlooking the courtyard, followed by coffee on the veranda. If dinner were in the evening, the moon might be seen rising over the beach and palms and reflected in the lagoon. When outdoor dining was inappropriate, the meal would be served in the dining room, with its display of Mrs. Bartlett's collection of china and Mr. Bartlett's collection of beer tankards from his beloved Munich where he studied as a young man.

Every aspect of Bonnet House radiated the Bartletts' relaxed lifestyle and enjoyment of beauty.

Favorite Recipes of the Bartletts

Caramelized Bacon

Thick bacon slices, cut into quarters
Brown sugar

Arrange the bacon slices in a single layer in a shallow baking pan.
Sprinkle the brown sugar over the bacon. Bake at 350 degrees for
15 minutes or until the bacon is brown. Remove and place on paper
towels to drain. Let stand until cool.

Yield: Variable

Rangpur Lime Cocktail

4   parts Barbados Eclipse dark rum
1   part fresh Rangpur lime juice
    Maple syrup

Combine the rum and lime juice in a pitcher and mix well. Add enough
syrup to sweeten to taste. Chill, covered, until ready to serve. Pour over
ice in a short glass.

Yield: Variable

The Rangpur lime
(Citrus limonia) is an
exotic tree imported
from India to Florida
in 1887. Its fruit is
small to medium in
size, more closely
resembling a mandarin
than a lime. A thin,
yellow-to-orange skin
covers the juicy
orange-red fruit inside.
It is one of the special
ingredients of Mrs.
Bartlett's own Rangpur
Lime Cocktail, a
drink she shared for
decades with friends at
Bonnet House, making
it a tradition.

French Watercress Soup

1	bunch watercress, rinsed	1	egg yolk
1	cup chicken broth	1	cup milk
1	small white onion, coarsely chopped	1¼	teaspoons sugar
		1	teaspoon ground nutmeg
1	small garlic clove	¼	teaspoon salt

Combine the watercress, broth, onion, garlic, egg yolk, milk, sugar, nutmeg and salt in a blender container. Process for 1 minute or until smooth. Pour into a saucepan. Heat over low heat until hot, stirring constantly.

Yield: 4 servings

Big Boss Oyster Soup

1	cup finely chopped celery	2	cups clam juice
1	cup finely chopped carrots	2	cups half-and-half
1	cup finely chopped white turnips	1	teaspoon flour
			Salt and pepper to taste
1	cup minced onion		Fresh chopped parsley
2	tablespoons butter or olive oil		for garnish
1	pint oysters with juice		

Sauté the celery, carrots, turnips and onion in the butter in a skillet. Remove the vegetables to a bowl. Add the oysters to the skillet and sauté until the edges curl. Add the vegetables and stir to combine. Add the clam juice and half-and-half gradually, stirring frequently. Dissolve the flour in a small amount of water in a cup. Stir into the oyster mixture. Cook until heated through, stirring frequently; do not boil. Season with salt and pepper. Ladle into soup bowls. Garnish with fresh chopped parsley.

Yield: 6 to 8 servings

Red Cabbage for Eight

2   heads red cabbage
2   tablespoons vinegar
1   onion, finely chopped
2   tablespoons bacon drippings
2   tablespoons butter
1   bay leaf
3   cloves
2   peppercorns
2   apples, thinly sliced
1   tablespoon butter
1   tablespoon flour
1   teaspoon sugar
    Juice of $1/2$ lemon

Rinse the cabbage and pat dry. Cut into thin slices. Combine the vinegar with enough water to cover the cabbage in a large bowl. Add the cabbage.

Cook the onion in the bacon drippings and 2 tablespoons butter in a skillet until browned. Drain the cabbage. Add to the onion. Add the bay leaf, cloves, peppercorns and apples. Cook over low heat until tender, stirring frequently.

Heat 1 tablespoon butter in a saucepan until melted. Stir in the flour. Add to the cabbage mixture, stirring until combined. Sprinkle the sugar and lemon juice over the cabbage mixture. Simmer for 1 to 2 minutes. Remove the bay leaf. Serve immediately.

Yield: 8 servings

While on a boat trip in Europe, Mrs. Bartlett was served a delicious oyster soup. She related the ingredients she was able to identify to her cook and was rewarded with a similarly delicious oyster soup prepared in her own kitchen. "Better than the soup on the ship," she told her cook.

Orange Roulade Dessert

6	eggs, at room temperature
1	cup sugar
1	cup flour
	Grated zest of 1 orange
4	cups heavy cream
1	cup sugar
3	tablespoons (about) Triple Sec
	Marmalade
	Toasted almonds

Combine the eggs and 1 cup sugar in the top of a double boiler. Place over simmering water. Cook until thickened, beating constantly at high speed. Beat in the flour gradually. Stir in the orange zest. Spoon into a 10×15-inch cake pan lined with waxed paper. Bake at 450 degrees for 12 minutes.

Dust a clean kitchen towel generously with confectioners' sugar. Invert the cake onto the towel. Remove the waxed paper and trim the edges. Roll the warm cake in the towel as for a jelly roll from the short side. Place on a wire rack to cool. Unroll the cooled cake carefully and remove the towel.

Beat the cream and 1 cup sugar in a bowl until soft peaks form. Add a small amount of the Triple Sec and mix well. Sprinkle the cake with the remaining Triple Sec. Spread a thin layer of marmalade to the edge. Spread the whipped cream mixture over the marmalade, reserving some of the whipped cream mixture to frost the cake. Reroll the cake. Decorate the top and side of the roll with the whipped cream mixture. Sprinkle the almonds over the cake. Wrap in plastic wrap. Chill until ready to serve. Cut into slices.

Yield: 8 servings

Peach Soufflé

1 (29-ounce) can cling peach slices
2 envelopes unflavored gelatin
2/3 cup sugar
2 egg yolks (see Editor's Note)
1 tablespoon lemon juice
1 teaspoon vanilla extract
1 cup ice cubes or crushed ice
2 egg whites
1/2 cup sugar
1 cup heavy cream
2 tablespoons peach brandy

Drain the peaches, reserving 1/2 cup of the syrup and 8 of the peach slices. Pour the reserved syrup into a blender container. Sprinkle the gelatin over the syrup. Let stand until softened. Add the remaining peaches, 2/3 cup sugar, egg yolks, lemon juice and vanilla. Process at high speed, adding the ice gradually and processing until the ice is melted. Pour into a large mixing bowl. Chill until the mixture mounds, stirring occasionally.

Beat the egg whites in a small bowl until soft peaks form. Add 1/2 cup sugar gradually, beating until stiff peaks form. Fold into the peach mixture.

Beat the cream in a large mixing bowl. Fold in the peach mixture and peach brandy. Pour into a 2-quart soufflé dish with a foil collar. Chill, covered, until set. Remove the collar and spoon into 8 dessert dishes. Garnish with the reserved peach slices.

Yield: 8 servings

Editor's Note: To avoid raw eggs that may carry salmonella, use an equivalent amount of pasteurized egg substitute, or meringue powder, sometimes sold as powdered egg whites.

The freshly baked
Molasses Ginger
Cookies were a
favorite snack of
Mr. Hugh Taylor
Birch. He was known
to often raid the cookie
jar and slip a few into
his pocket.

Molasses Ginger Cookies

2 cups sifted flour	3/4 cup shortening
2 teaspoons baking soda	1 cup sugar
1 teaspoon cinnamon	1/4 cup molasses, cane sugar or
1/2 teaspoon ginger	packed brown sugar
1/2 teaspoon cloves	1 egg, beaten
1/2 teaspoon salt	

Sift the flour, baking soda, cinnamon, ginger, cloves and salt together.
Cream the shortening, sugar and molasses in a mixing bowl until light
and fluffy. Add the egg and mix well. Add the dry ingredients and mix
well. Shape into 1-inch balls. Place 2 inches apart on a greased cookie
sheet. Bake at 350 degrees for 10 to 12 minutes. Cool on a wire rack.

Yield: 4 dozen cookies

Peanut Butter Strips

1 loaf white bread	3/4 cup corn oil
1 (12-ounce) jar creamy peanut	1 tablespoon sugar
butter	

Cut the bread into 1/2-inch-thick slices. Trim the bread, reserving the
crusts. Process the crusts into fine crumbs in a food processor fitted with a
steel blade. Spread the bread crumbs over a baking sheet. Bake at 275
degrees for 15 minutes. Place in a shallow dish. Cut each bread slice into
6 strips. Arrange in a single layer on a baking sheet. Bake at 275 degrees
for 45 minutes. Place the peanut butter, corn oil and sugar in the top of
a double boiler. Cook over simmering water until heated through and
smooth, stirring frequently. Dip each bread strip in the peanut butter
mixture. Roll in the bread crumbs to coat. Place on waxed paper to cool.
Store in an airtight container.

Yield: Variable

Brunch

Linens, silverware, china,

and delightful centerpieces

were coordinated to match

the mood and menu.

Sponsored by
Gill Hotels

Breakfast for two on the balcony overlooking a giant banyan tree is set with Evelyn Bartlett's beloved blue and white china, hibiscus, and seagrape leaves.

Apple Bananas and Sea Fan,
watercolor by Evelyn Bartlett.

A brunch table is set in the dramatic
arched entrance to the Courtyard Fountain.
In the background is the archway to
Mr. Bartlett's north-lit studio.

Andrew Itkoff

Theodore Flagg

Pineapple and avocado with white compote, *painting by Mrs. Bartlett.*

Tony Branco ©

East gate
*The wrought iron gates open to a
shell road lined with melaleuca trees,
which leads to the oasis inside.*

Table of Contents

Sponsored by
Kitchens to Go

Minted Peach Melon Soup

1   pound peaches, peeled, sliced
1   small cantaloupe, chopped (about 4 cups)
    Juice of 1 lime
10 to 12 finely minced mint leaves
    Yogurt or sour cream for garnish
    Mint sprigs for garnish

Purée the peaches, cantaloupe and lime juice in a food processor. Stir in the mint leaves. Chill, covered, for 3 hours or longer. Spoon into glass bowls. Garnish with yogurt and mint sprigs.

Yield: 6 servings

Mucho Gusto Gazpacho

1   (46-ounce) can vegetable juice cocktail
33   ounces spicy hot vegetable juice cocktail
3/4 cup finely chopped seeded peeled cucumber
1/2 cup finely chopped celery
1/2 cup finely chopped red or yellow bell pepper
1/2 cup finely chopped green bell pepper
1   medium onion, finely chopped
12   black olives, chopped
12   green olives, chopped
1   teaspoon garlic powder
2   tablespoons vegetable oil
     Sour cream for garnish

Combine the vegetable juice cocktail, cucumber, celery, bell peppers, onion, olives, garlic powder and vegetable oil in a large bowl and mix well. Chill, covered, for 8 to 12 hours to enhance the flavors. Ladle into soup bowls. Garnish with sour cream. May be served hot or cold.

Yield: 12 servings

Bleu Cheese Crisps

2   (4-ounce) packages crumbled bleu cheese
$^1/_2$ cup (1 stick) butter, softened
$1^1/_3$ cups flour
$^1/_3$ cup poppy seeds
$^1/_4$ teaspoon cayenne pepper

Beat the bleu cheese and butter in a mixing bowl at medium speed until light and fluffy. Add the flour, poppy seeds and cayenne pepper and mix well. Divide the dough into 2 equal portions. Shape each portion into a 9-inch log. Wrap in plastic wrap. Chill for 2 hours or longer. Cut the logs into $^1/_4$-inch slices. Place on a baking sheet. Bake at 350 degrees for 13 to 15 minutes or until golden brown. Cool on a wire rack.

Yield: 6 dozen

Herb-Stuffed Mushrooms

2   pounds medium-large mushrooms, rinsed
$1^1/_4$ cups ($2^1/_2$ sticks) butter
1   cup finely chopped green onions
1   cup white wine
4   cups herb-seasoned stuffing mix

Remove the stems from the mushrooms, reserving the stems. Arrange the mushroom caps in a shallow baking dish. Chop the reserved mushroom stems. Heat the butter in a large skillet until melted. Add the mushroom stems and green onions. Sauté until tender. Stir in the wine and stuffing mix. Spoon the stuffing mixture into the mushroom caps. Bake at 350 degrees for 25 to 30 minutes.

Yield: Approximately 40 mushrooms

Brunch

Island Coconut Chips with Island Seasoning

1   fresh coconut, cracked, drained
1   teaspoon Island Seasoning

Remove the coconut meat from the outer shell. Remove the brown surface skin. Peel coconut meat into long wide strips. Arrange on a foil-lined baking sheet. Sprinkle with Island Seasoning. Bake at 375 degrees until lightly browned.

Yield: Variable

Island Seasoning

1   tablespoon allspice
1   tablespoon nutmeg
1   tablespoon cloves
1¹/₂ teaspoons cinnamon
1¹/₂ teaspoons mace
1   teaspoon thyme
1   teaspoon freshly ground pepper

Combine the allspice, nutmeg, cloves, cinnamon, mace, thyme and pepper in a bowl and mix well. Store in an airtight container in a dry cool place. May also use on grilled fish, chicken or steamed vegetables.

When Frederic Bartlett married Helen Birch in 1919, her father, Hugh Taylor Birch, gave the newlyweds a "house lot" on Fort Lauderdale beach. The size? "Oh, about as far as you can swing a cat," said Birch. He must have had a good swing—the original size was 35 acres.

Brunch

Peanut Chutney Spread

1	cup chunky peanut butter	1	teaspoon Worcestershire
3	ounces cream cheese		sauce
1	(9-ounce) jar Major Grey chutney		Sherry to taste

Place the peanut butter and cream cheese in a microwave-safe bowl. Microwave for 30 to 60 seconds or until softened. Add the chutney, Worcestershire sauce and enough sherry to make of a spreading consistency and mix well. Serve with Melba toast, crackers or apple slices.

Yield: 30 servings

Salmon Pâté

1	(16-ounce) can salmon	1/2	teaspoon liquid smoke (optional)
1/3	cup minced onion		
8	ounces cream cheese, softened	1 1/4	teaspoons Worcestershire sauce
3	tablespoons fresh lemon juice (juice of about 1 lemon)	2	dashes (or more) of red pepper sauce
4 1/2	teaspoons (or more) drained horseradish		Salt and pepper to taste
2 1/2	teaspoons dill		Lemon wedges for garnish
1/4	cup chopped fresh parsley		Parsley for garnish

Drain the salmon and remove any skin, bones or fat. Process the salmon, onion, cream cheese, lemon juice, horseradish, dill, 1/4 cup parsley, liquid smoke, Worcestershire sauce, red pepper sauce, salt and pepper in a food processor fitted with a steel blade until smooth, adding additional horseradish and red pepper sauce if desired. Spoon into a serving bowl or onto a bed of lettuce on a serving plate. Garnish with lemon wedges and parsley. Serve with crackers, cocktail rye bread or sliced vegetables.

Yield: 10 to 12 servings

Little Harbor Conch Fritters

1	pound conch, coarsely chopped	2	teaspoons red hot sauce
1	bell pepper, minced	1	teaspoon thyme
1	onion, minced	1	cup baking mix
3	garlic cloves, minced	2	eggs
1	tablespoon minced parsley	1/4	cup milk
	Grated zest of 1 lime or lemon		Vegetable oil for frying
			Papaya Mustard Sauce

Pound the conch with a meat mallet to tenderize if desired. Finely chop in a food processor fitted with a steel blade. Combine the conch, bell pepper, onion, garlic, parsley, lime zest, red hot sauce, thyme, baking mix, eggs and milk in a bowl and mix well. Chill, covered, for 1 hour or longer. Heat the vegetable oil in a skillet. Drop the dough by spoonfuls into the hot oil. Fry until brown on both sides, turning once. Remove and place on paper towels to drain. Serve with Papaya Mustard Sauce.

Yield: 10 to 12 servings

Papaya Mustard Sauce

1	papaya or mango, peeled, seeded, chopped	2	tablespoons brown sugar
1	tomato, chopped	2	tablespoons Worcestershire sauce
1/2	cup chopped red onion	1	teaspoon red hot sauce
2	jalapeño chiles, seeded, minced	1/2	teaspoon allspice
1/2	cup red wine vinegar	1/4	teaspoon freshly ground pepper
1/4	cup dry white wine	1/4	teaspoon salt
2	tablespoons Dijon mustard		

Combine the papaya, tomato, red onion, jalapeño chiles, vinegar, wine, mustard, brown sugar, Worcestershire sauce, red hot sauce, allspice, pepper and salt in a nonreactive saucepan. Cook over low heat, stirring frequently. Bring to a simmer. Simmer for 10 to 12 minutes or until the mixture is the consistency of jam. Remove from the heat. Let stand until cool. You may process the sauce in a blender for a smoother consistency. Serve immediately or store in the refrigerator for up to 2 weeks.

Killer Shrimp

Frederic drew up
plans for the original
house as well as for
architectural additions.
He had a workshop
on the property where
he created decorative
touches to enhance
the basic house.

Salt to taste
3 pounds medium shrimp
1/4 cup chopped parsley
1/4 cup finely chopped shallots or green onions
1/4 cup tarragon vinegar
1/4 cup wine vinegar
1/4 cup olive oil
1/4 cup Dijon mustard
2 teaspoons crushed red pepper
2 teaspoons salt
Freshly ground black pepper to taste

Bring enough water to cover the shrimp to a boil in a saucepan. Add salt to taste. Add the shrimp and cook until shrimp turn pink. Drain and peel the shrimp. Place the warm shrimp in a sealable plastic bag. Combine the parsley, shallots, tarragon vinegar, wine vinegar, olive oil, mustard, red pepper, 2 teaspoons salt and black pepper in a bowl and mix well. Pour over the warm shrimp, turning to coat; seal. Chill for 3 hours or longer. Drain and place in a serving bowl.

Yield: 8 to 10 servings

"Brunch on the Veranda" French Toast with Blue Mountain Syrup

1   loaf sliced cinnamon-raisin bread
6   cups milk
1   (8-ounce) can coconut cream
6   eggs, beaten
3   tablespoons sugar
1   teaspoon freshly grated nutmeg
1   teaspoon vanilla extract
    Blue Mountain Syrup

Layer the bread slices in a 9×13-inch baking dish, overlapping as needed. Combine the milk, coconut cream, eggs, sugar, nutmeg and vanilla in a bowl and mix well. Pour over the bread. Chill, tightly covered, for 8 to 12 hours. Bake at 350 degrees for 1 hour. Serve with Blue Mountain Syrup.

Yield: 8 to 10 servings

Blue Mountain Syrup

1   (8-ounce) bottle pure maple syrup
2   tablespoons Tía Maria liqueur

Combine the maple syrup and Tía Maria liqueur in a pitcher and mix well. You may warm the syrup if desired.

Brunch

Never-Fail Bread and Cheese Soufflé

16	ounces sharp Cheddar cheese, shredded
6	eggs, lightly beaten
2¹/4	cups milk
2	tablespoons mustard
2	tablespoons minced green onions
2	teaspoons brown sugar
¹/2	teaspoon Worcestershire sauce
¹/2	teaspoon salt
	Dash of cayenne pepper
10	slices firm-textured dried bread, trimmed, cubed

Combine the Cheddar cheese, eggs, milk, mustard, green onions, brown sugar, Worcestershire sauce, salt and cayenne pepper in a bowl and mix well. Alternate layers of the bread cubes and cheese mixture in a greased shallow 2-quart baking dish until all of the ingredients are used, ending with the cheese mixture.

Chill, covered, for 6 to 12 hours. Bake in a preheated 325-degree oven for 50 to 55 minutes or until set.

Yield: 8 servings

Blintz Soufflé

8	ounces cream cheese, softened	$1/2$	cup orange juice
2	cups small curd cottage cheese	$1/2$	cup (1 stick) butter or margarine, softened
2	egg yolks	1	cup flour
1	tablespoon sugar	$1/3$	cup sugar
1	teaspoon vanilla extract	2	teaspoons baking powder
6	eggs	1	teaspoon grated orange zest
$1^1/2$	cups sour cream		Blueberry Sauce

Combine the cream cheese, cottage cheese, egg yolks, 1 tablespoon sugar and vanilla in a mixing bowl. Beat at medium speed until smooth.

Process the eggs, sour cream, orange juice and butter in a blender until smooth. Add the flour, $1/3$ cup sugar, baking powder and orange zest. Process until smooth. Pour half of the batter into a greased 9×13-inch baking dish. Spoon the cream cheese mixture evenly over the batter. Spread to cover the batter in the prepared dish. Pour the remaining batter over the cream cheese mixture. Bake at 350 degrees for 50 to 60 minutes or until puffed and golden brown. Serve immediately with Blueberry Sauce.

Yield: 8 to 10 servings

Blueberry Sauce

$2/3$	cup sugar	1	cup water
2	tablespoons cornstarch	2	cups fresh blueberries
	Dash of cinnamon	2	tablespoons lemon juice
	Dash of nutmeg		

Combine the sugar, cornstarch, cinnamon and nutmeg in a heavy saucepan and mix well. Stir in the water gradually. Bring to a boil over medium heat, stirring constantly. Boil for 1 minute. Stir in the blueberries and lemon juice. Remove from the heat and serve immediately.

Bonnet House stands on a barrier island that began as a chain of sandbars shaped by ocean currents and was eventually covered by shrubs and trees. It extended from north to south, cut by inlets, and served as a barrier between the Atlantic Ocean and the mainland.

33

Brunch

Cheesy Egg Casserole

1   (20-slice) loaf white bread, trimmed, cubed
1/4 cup (1/2 stick) butter, melted
1 1/2 cups shredded Swiss cheese
1/4 cup shredded Monterey Jack cheese
1   pound bacon, crisp-cooked, crumbled
8   eggs
1 2/3 cups milk
1/4 cup dry white wine
2   green onions, minced
1   tablespoon Dijon mustard
1   cup sour cream
1   cup grated Parmesan cheese

Sprinkle the bread cubes evenly over the bottom of a greased 9×13-inch baking dish. Drizzle the butter over the bread. Sprinkle with the Swiss and Monterey Jack cheeses. Sprinkle the bacon over the cheeses. Whisk the eggs, milk, wine, green onions and mustard in a bowl. Pour over the layers.

Chill, covered, for 6 to 24 hours. Let stand at room temperature for 30 minutes. Bake, covered with foil, at 325 degrees for 1 hour or until set.

Combine the sour cream and Parmesan cheese in a bowl and mix well. Spread over the top. Bake, uncovered, for an additional 10 minutes or until the top is crusty and light brown.

Yield: 8 servings

Brunch

Mushroom Tart

1 unbaked (9-inch) pie shell
2 cups thinly sliced mushrooms (about 8 ounces)
2 tablespoons butter or margarine
2 cups shredded Swiss cheese (about 8 ounces)
4 eggs
1 1/2 cups half-and-half
1/4 teaspoon white pepper
1/4 teaspoon nutmeg

Fit the pie shell into a tart pan, pie plate or quiche dish. Chill, covered, until ready to use.

Sauté the mushrooms in the butter in a skillet until golden brown; drain. Sprinkle the cheese evenly over the bottom of the pastry. Arrange the mushrooms over the cheese. Beat the eggs, half-and-half, white pepper and nutmeg in a medium bowl until well mixed but not frothy. Pour over the mushrooms.

Bake at 375 degrees for 40 to 45 minutes or until the top is golden brown and the center is firm. Serve immediately or at room temperature.

Yield: 6 to 8 servings

Oolite limestone, primarily made of stony corals and fossilized organisms, is indigenous to the Florida Keys. Frederic selected it for the walks and obelisks at Bonnet House. This hardened limestone is now prized as a valuable building material.

Crowd Pleaser Casserole

At one time, Mr. Birch had salvaged a huge mahogany log from the beach. He gave this to Frederic, who then used its boards in the ceiling of the drawing room.

2   pounds bulk sausage
1   cup shredded sharp Cheddar cheese
4   eggs, beaten
1   cup cooked grits
1   (8-ounce) package corn muffin mix
1³/4 cups hot milk
¹/2 cup (1 stick) butter, melted
1   cup shredded sharp Cheddar cheese

Brown the sausage in a skillet, stirring until crumbly; drain. Layer the sausage and 1 cup Cheddar cheese over the bottom of a greased 2-quart baking dish. Combine the eggs, grits, corn muffin mix, hot milk and butter in a bowl and mix well.

Pour the egg mixture over the prepared layers. Sprinkle 1 cup Cheddar cheese over the top. You may chill the casserole, covered, at this point for 8 to 12 hours. Bake at 325 degrees for 45 minutes.

Yield: 6 to 8 servings

Creamed Chipped Beef

1 1/2 pounds fresh mushrooms
1   large onion, chopped
1/2 cup (1 stick) butter
6   (2-ounce) jars dried beef, cut into thin strips
1/2 cup flour
3   cups skim milk

Remove and discard the mushroom stems. Cut the mushrooms into quarters. Sauté with the onion in the butter in a skillet. Remove the mushrooms and onion and set aside.

Place the beef in the skillet. Cook until lightly browned, stirring frequently. Sprinkle the flour over the beef and stir until combined. Reduce the heat to low.

Pour the milk into the skillet gradually, stirring constantly. Cook until the sauce is thickened and smooth, stirring constantly. Stir in the reserved mushrooms and onion. Cook until heated through. Serve over biscuits or baked potatoes. You may freeze this dish.

Yield: 12 to 15 servings

The fruit grove at Bonnet House, cultivated by Mr. Birch and the Bartletts, produced avocado, sapodilla, guava, rose apple, Surinam cherry, calabash, and grapefruit, all of which appeared as delicacies prepared by the house chef.

37

The Melaleuca, or Cajeput Trees, were planted by Frederic Bartlett to line the entrance road of Bonnet House. Now at magnificent heights, the trees were initially imported from Australia to Florida because they soaked up water through their root systems and converted swamp to farmland. Melaleucas are now controlled to save native vegetation and water.

Brunch

Bronzed Tuna

1/4   cup (1/2 stick) butter or margarine
2   (1-inch-thick) tuna steaks
      (about 8 to 12 ounces each)
1   tablespoon Chef Paul Prudhomme's
      Blackened Redfish Magic®

Heat the butter in a nonstick skillet until melted. Add the tuna and quickly coat both sides thoroughly with the butter. Remove from the skillet. Wipe the skillet dry. Heat over high heat for 4 minutes.

Sprinkle one side of the tuna with the Redfish Magic®. Place spiced side down in the hot skillet. Cook for 1 1/2 minutes.

Sprinkle the top with the Redfish Magic®. Turn the tuna. Cook for 15 to 20 seconds; tuna will be rare. May be served cold or sliced on a Caesar salad.

Yield: 2 servings

Golden Shrimp Puff

4	eggs
2	cups milk
1^1/$_2$	tablespoons minced parsley
^{1}/$_2$	teaspoon dry mustard
^{1}/$_4$	teaspoon salt
5	bread slices, trimmed, cubed
1	cup shredded sharp cheese
1^1/$_2$	cups cooked shrimp, chopped

Beat the eggs, milk, parsley, mustard and salt in a bowl. Stir in the bread cubes, cheese and shrimp. Spoon into a greased 7×11-inch baking dish. Bake at 325 degrees for 1 hour or until puffed and golden brown.

Yield: 8 servings

Pineapple au Gratin

2	(20-ounce) cans pineapple chunks, drained
1	cup sugar
6	tablespoons flour
2	cups shredded sharp Cheddar cheese
32	butter crackers, crumbled
^{1}/$_2$	cup (1 stick) butter, melted

Combine the pineapple, sugar, flour and cheese in a bowl and mix well. Spoon into a greased 2-quart baking dish. Sprinkle the cracker crumbs over the pineapple mixture. Drizzle with the melted butter. Bake at 350 degrees for 25 minutes.

Yield: 8 to 10 servings

In the 1930s, Evelyn Bartlett planted the now majestic Florida Royal Palms along the lagoon in front of Bonnet House, using birthday money given to her by her father. In the late 1980s, she planted new seedlings between the existing palms to maintain the view.

Brunch

Mango Tango Salad

Orange Lemon Dressing
6 cups shredded cabbage
1/2 cup sliced scallions
1/3 cup chopped parsley
1 mango, peeled, chopped
1/3 cup sliced almonds

Combine the Orange Lemon Dressing, cabbage, scallions, parsley and mango in a large bowl and toss to combine. Chill, covered, for 2 to 8 hours. Sprinkle the almonds over the top.

Yield: 6 to 8 servings

Orange Lemon Dressing

1/2 cup light mayonnaise
2 tablespoons orange juice
1 tablespoon lemon juice
1 tablespoon rice vinegar
1 teaspoon salt
1/8 teaspoon cayenne pepper

Combine the mayonnaise, orange juice, lemon juice, vinegar, salt and cayenne pepper in a bowl and mix well.

40

Lemony Mint Pasta Salad

1   (12-ounce) package lemon pepper linguini
    Olive oil
1/3 cup sliced green onions
1/4 teaspoon salt
1/8 teaspoon freshly ground pepper
1   tablespoon Dijon mustard
3   or 4 sprigs of mint
    Lime Mint Vinaigrette

Cook the pasta using the package directions; drain. Combine the pasta
with a small amount of olive oil and toss to combine. Add the green
onions, salt, pepper, mustard and mint and mix well. Add Lime Mint
Vinaigrette and toss to combine.

Yield: 6 to 8 servings

Lime Mint Vinaigrette

1   tablespoon grated lime zest
3   tablespoons lime juice
4 1/2 teaspoons rice vinegar
    Salt and pepper to taste
1/2 cup olive oil
1/4 cup chopped fresh mint
1/2 teaspoon sugar (optional)

Place the lime zest, lime juice, vinegar, salt, pepper, olive oil and mint in
a jar with a cover. Cover the jar and shake until combined. Stir in the
sugar if the dressing is too tart.

Brunch

A Festive Spinach and Strawberry Salad

8	cups fresh spinach leaves, stems removed
1	pint fresh strawberries, cut into halves
1	cup sugar
1	cup canola oil
$1/2$	cup cider vinegar
$1/4$	cup sesame seeds
$1/4$	cup poppy seeds
1	teaspoon paprika
1	teaspoon Worcestershire sauce
1	teaspoon minced onion
$1/2$	teaspoon dry mustard

Combine the spinach and strawberries in a salad bowl. Combine the sugar, canola oil, vinegar, sesame seeds, poppy seeds, paprika, Worcestershire sauce, onion and mustard in a blender container and process until well mixed. Pour over the salad and toss to combine.

Yield: 6 to 8 servings

Brunch

Tangy Marinated Squash

5	medium yellow squash, thinly sliced
1/2	cup sliced green onions
1/2	cup chopped green bell pepper
1/2	cup chopped celery
3/4	cup sugar
1	teaspoon salt
1/2	teaspoon pepper
1/3	cup salad oil
2/3	cup cider vinegar
2	tablespoons red wine vinegar
1	garlic clove, crushed

Place the squash, green onions, bell pepper and celery in a bowl. Combine the sugar, salt, pepper, salad oil, cider vinegar, red wine vinegar and garlic in a small bowl and mix well. Pour over the vegetables, tossing to coat. Chill, covered, for 12 hours, stirring occasionally. Drain and place in a serving bowl.

Yield: 6 servings

The mangrove swamp on Bonnet House property that borders the Intracoastal Waterway is a valuable ecosystem. This endangered wetland shelters micro-organisms that form a food chain for shrimp and small fish, which are then prey for large fish. Law protects it.

Brunch

Tropical Fiesta Salad

1	cup snow peas
12	ounces shrimp, deveined, cooked
1	mango, peeled, chopped
1/4	cup sliced green onions
1/2	red bell pepper, thinly sliced
1/2	red onion, thinly sliced
	Lime Mango Vinaigrette to taste
	Lettuce leaves

Bring enough water to cover the snow peas to a boil in a saucepan. Add the snow peas. Boil for 2 minutes; drain. Place the snow peas, shrimp, mango, green onions, bell pepper and red onion in a bowl. Add Lime Mango Vinaigrette and toss to combine. Serve over lettuce leaves.

Yield: 6 servings

Lime Mango Vinaigrette

1	tablespoon grated lime zest
3	tablespoons fresh lime juice
4 1/2	teaspoons rice vinegar
1/4	teaspoon salt
	Freshly ground black pepper
1/2	cup mild olive oil
1/4	cup finely chopped mango
1/4	cup chopped fresh mint

Place the lime zest, lime juice, vinegar, salt, pepper, olive oil, mango and mint in a jar with a cover. Cover the jar and shake until combined.

Brunch

Apricot Bread

1¹/₂ cups dried apricots	1 tablespoon baking powder
¹/₂ cup (1 stick) butter, softened	¹/₄ teaspoon baking soda
1 cup sugar	³/₄ teaspoon salt
2 eggs, beaten	1 teaspoon grated orange zest
³/₄ cup orange juice	1 cup chopped walnuts
2 cups flour, sifted	

Cut the apricots into bite-size pieces. Place in a bowl and add enough water to cover. Let stand for 30 minutes; drain and chop. Cream the butter and sugar in a mixing bowl until light and fluffy. Add the eggs alternately with the orange juice, mixing well after each addition. Add the flour, baking powder, baking soda and salt and mix well. Stir in the apricots, orange zest and walnuts. Pour into a greased 5×9-inch loaf pan. Bake at 350 degrees for 1¹/₂ hours.

Yield: 12 servings

Heirloom Banana Bread

¹/₂ cup (1 stick) butter, softened	¹/₂ teaspoon salt
2 cups sugar	2 teaspoons cinnamon
2 eggs	1 teaspoon cloves
2 cups mashed bananas	¹/₂ cup buttermilk
(about 4 or 5 bananas)	³/₄ cup chopped walnuts
3 cups flour	¹/₂ cup golden raisins
1¹/₂ teaspoons baking soda	

Combine the butter, sugar, eggs, bananas, flour, baking soda, salt, cinnamon, cloves and buttermilk in a bowl and mix well. Fold in the walnuts and raisins. Spoon into 2 loaf pans sprayed with nonstick cooking spray. Bake at 350 degrees for 1 hour. Cool in the pans. You may substitute ¹/₂ cup milk mixed with 1 tablespoon vinegar for the buttermilk.

Yield: 24 servings

45

Whole Wheat Banana Bread

1   cup sifted all-purpose flour
1   teaspoon baking powder
1   teaspoon baking soda
$1/4$ teaspoon salt
$1/4$ teaspoon freshly ground nutmeg (optional)
$1/2$ teaspoon cinnamon
1   cup whole wheat flour
$1/2$ cup (1 stick) butter or margarine, softened
$1/2$ cup packed brown sugar
1   egg, lightly beaten
3   bananas, mashed (about $1^1/4$ cups)
$1/4$ cup yogurt or sour cream
$1/2$ cup chopped nuts (optional)

Sift the all-purpose flour, baking powder, baking soda, salt, nutmeg and cinnamon into a medium bowl. Stir in the whole wheat flour. Cream the butter and brown sugar in a large bowl until light and fluffy. Add the egg, bananas and yogurt and mix well. Add the flour mixture and chopped nuts and mix just until blended. Spoon into a greased loaf pan.

Bake at 350 degrees for 55 minutes or until a wooden pick inserted in the center comes out clean. Cool in the pan for 10 minutes. Remove to a wire rack to cool completely.

Yield: 12 servings

Brunch

Mango Bread

2   cups flour
2   teaspoons baking soda
2   teaspoons cinnamon
1/2   teaspoon salt
1/2   cup raisins
1/2   cup walnuts, chopped (optional)
2   eggs
1   cup sugar
1/2   cup vegetable oil
1/4   cup honey
1/2   teaspoon vanilla extract
2   cups slightly mashed mango

Sift the flour, baking soda, cinnamon and salt into a medium bowl. Stir in the raisins and walnuts. Beat the eggs in a large mixing bowl until frothy. Add the sugar and oil and mix well. Beat in the honey and vanilla gradually. Stir in the mango. Add the flour mixture and stir just until blended. Pour into 2 greased and floured 5×9-inch loaf pans. Let stand for 20 minutes.

Bake at 350 degrees for 50 to 60 minutes or until a wooden pick inserted in the center comes out clean. Cool in the pans for 10 minutes. Invert onto a wire rack to cool completely.

Yield: 2 loaves

Garden walks with a local garden columnist are a popular part of the Bonnet House program. Garden clubs maintain an interest in Bonnet House activities. Spring and summer classes by the orchid curator are popular. Specialists from the nearby Hugh Taylor Birch State Park also give lectures. The education program offers tours for schoolchildren, in which they learn about the barrier islands upon which the Bonnet House is built and its unique trees, plants, and animals.

Nibble Bread

The Bartletts' main residence, Whitehall, was located in Beverly, Massachusetts. Evelyn Bartlett also maintained a 114-acre farm, Bothways, in nearby Essex.

6	ounces cream cheese, softened
1/3	cup sugar
1	tablespoon flour
1	egg
1	teaspoon grated orange zest
1	egg, beaten
1/2	cup orange juice
1/2	cup water
1	(15-ounce) package quick bread mix of choice

Combine the cream cheese, sugar and flour in a bowl and mix well. Beat in 1 egg and orange zest.

Combine the beaten egg, orange juice and water in a bowl and mix well. Add the quick bread mix, stirring just until moistened. Pour 2/3 of the batter into a greased and floured 5×9-inch loaf pan. Spoon the cream cheese mixture evenly over the batter. Spoon the remaining batter over the cream cheese mixture.

Bake at 350 degrees for 1 hour. Cool in the pan for 10 minutes. Remove to a wire rack to cool completely. Chill, covered, for 8 to 12 hours.

Yield: 12 servings

Pull-Apart Bread

$^1/_2$ cup chopped pecans
18 to 20 frozen white bread rolls
1 (4-ounce) package butterscotch cook-and-serve
    pudding mix
$^1/_2$ cup packed brown sugar
$^1/_2$ cup (1 stick) butter
1 teaspoon cinnamon
$^1/_2$ cup chopped pecans

Sprinkle $^1/_2$ cup chopped pecans over the bottom of a bundt pan sprayed with nonstick cooking spray. Arrange the rolls evenly in the pan. Sprinkle the pudding mix over the rolls.

Combine the brown sugar, butter and cinnamon in a saucepan. Cook until the butter is melted, stirring occasionally. Pour over the pudding mix. Sprinkle $^1/_2$ cup chopped pecans over the top. Cover with a towel. Let stand for 8 to 12 hours.

Bake at 350 degrees for 25 to 30 minutes or until bread tests done. Cool in the pan for 15 to 20 minutes. Run a knife around the edge to loosen. Invert onto a serving plate. Pull apart to serve.

Yield: 10 to 12 servings

Evelyn's farm in Massachusetts produced meat and poultry, eggs, vegetables, milk, and cream, much of which was consumed in Massachusetts and Florida. Every two weeks a shipment of foodstuffs from the farm was delivered to Bonnet House. Animals would have been slaughtered and the meat frozen for use in both places, with Mrs. Bartlett carefully marking the packages as to contents and weight.

Piña Colada Muffins

1	(2-layer) package yellow or butter-recipe cake mix
1	teaspoon coconut extract
1	teaspoon rum extract
1	cup flaked coconut
1/2	to 1 cup chopped nuts
1	(8-ounce) can crushed pineapple

Prepare the cake mix using the package directions. Add the coconut extract, rum extract, coconut, nuts and undrained pineapple and mix for 1 minute; do not overmix. Fill greased miniature muffin cups 3/4 full. Bake at 350 degrees for 15 to 20 minutes or until the muffins test done.

Yield: 22 to 25 muffins

Lemon Raisin Scones

1	egg
1	cup lemon yogurt
2 1/2	cups flour
1/4	cup sugar
2	teaspoons baking powder
1	teaspoon baking soda
1	teaspoon grated lemon zest
1/4	cup (1/2 stick) butter
1/2	cup raisins

Combine the egg and yogurt in a bowl and mix well. Combine the flour, sugar, baking powder, baking soda and lemon zest in a large bowl and mix well. Cut in the butter until crumbly. Stir in the raisins. Pour in the yogurt mixture and mix just until moistened. Drop by spoonfuls onto a greased baking sheet. Bake at 425 degrees for 11 to 14 minutes or until golden brown. Serve warm with butter, jam or lemon curd.

Yield: 12 to 14 servings

Brunch

Fast and Easy Fruit Sorbet

1   (20-ounce) can syrup-pack fruit
3   tablespoons vodka, rum or liqueur
1/2 cup fresh berries, or 1 banana (optional)
    Fresh mint or berries for garnish

Freeze the can of fruit until firm. Let stand at room temperature for
30 minutes. Open the can at both ends and push fruit into the container
of a food processor. Add the vodka and berries. Process until smooth.
Spoon into serving dishes and serve immediately. May be frozen in
serving dishes until ready to serve. Garnish with fresh mint or berries.

Yield: 4 to 6 servings

The Best, Most Moist Pound Cake

1 1/2 cups (3 sticks) butter, softened
3   cups sugar
6   eggs
3   cups flour
1   tablespoon baking powder
1   cup milk
1   teaspoon almond extract
1   teaspoon vanilla extract

Cream the butter and sugar in a mixing bowl until light and fluffy. Add
the eggs 1 at a time, mixing well after each addition. Add the flour and
baking powder and mix well. Beat in the milk, almond extract and
vanilla gradually. Beat at high speed for 15 to 18 minutes. Pour into a
greased and floured bundt pan. Bake at 350 degrees for 1 1/4 hours. Cool
in the pan. Invert onto a serving plate. Do not use skim or low-fat milk
in this recipe.

Yield: 15 servings

51

Florida Pecan Bundt Cake

Evelyn loved her Massachusetts farm and would have great long conversations with her friend and fellow farmer, Jack Wilcox, when he called her every Sunday.

3	cups cake flour, sifted
2	teaspoons baking powder
1	teaspoon salt
1/2	teaspoon freshly grated nutmeg
1	cup shortening
2 1/2	cups sugar
6	eggs
1	cup sour cream
1/2	cup bourbon
1	cup finely chopped pecans, toasted
	Bourbon Glaze
	Pecan halves for decoration

Sift the flour, baking powder, salt and nutmeg together. Beat the shortening and sugar in a mixing bowl until light and fluffy. Add the eggs 1 at a time, mixing well after each addition. Add the sifted dry ingredients alternately with the sour cream and bourbon, beginning and ending with the dry ingredients and mixing well after each addition. Fold in the chopped pecans. Pour into a greased and floured 10-inch tube or bundt pan.

Bake at 325 degrees for 1 1/4 hours or until a wooden pick inserted in the center comes out clean. Cool in the pan for 15 minutes. Invert onto a wire rack to cool completely. Place on a cake plate. Spread Bourbon Glaze over the cooled cake. Decorate with the pecan halves.

Yield: 16 servings

Bourbon Glaze

2	cups sifted confectioners' sugar
1	tablespoon bourbon
2	tablespoons (about) water

Combine the confectioners' sugar, bourbon and enough water to make of a spreading consistency in a bowl and mix well.

My Mom's Pineapple Cake

2   cups sugar
2   cups flour
2   teaspoons baking soda
1   (20-ounce) can crushed pineapple
2   eggs
1   teaspoon vanilla extract
    Cream Cheese Glaze

Combine the sugar, flour, baking soda, undrained pineapple, eggs and vanilla in a bowl and mix well. Pour into a 9×13-inch baking pan.

Bake at 350 degrees for 35 to 40 minutes or until the cake is brown and pulls from the sides of the pan. Let stand until cool. Spread Cream Cheese Glaze over the top. Chill, covered, until the glaze is set.

Yield: 15 servings

Cream Cheese Glaze

8   ounces cream cheese, softened
$1/2$ cup (1 stick) butter, softened
1   teaspoon vanilla extract
$1^1/3$ cups confectioners' sugar

Beat the cream cheese and butter in a bowl until smooth. Beat in the vanilla. Add the confectioners' sugar gradually and beat until smooth; the glaze will be thin.

53

Blueberry Torte

1	cup sugar	2	eggs
1/2	cup (1 stick) butter, softened	1	to 2 cups blueberries, rinsed
1	cup unbleached flour		Sugar to taste
1	teaspoon baking powder	1	tablespoon lemon juice
	Pinch of salt	3/4	teaspoon cinnamon

Cream 1 cup sugar and butter in a mixing bowl until light and fluffy.
Add the flour, baking powder, salt and eggs and mix well. Pour into a
springform pan. Pat the blueberries dry. Sprinkle evenly over the batter.
Sprinkle the sugar to taste, lemon juice and cinnamon evenly over the
blueberries. Bake at 350 degrees for 45 to 60 minutes or until the torte
tests done. Let stand until slightly cooled. Remove the side of the pan.
Serve with ice cream. You may substitute raspberries for the blueberries.

Yield: 8 servings

Orange Crisps

1	loaf thinly sliced white bread	1	cup sugar
1	cup (2 sticks) butter		Grated zest of 2 oranges

Trim the crusts from the bread. Combine the butter, sugar and orange zest
in a saucepan. Cook until the butter is melted and the mixture is heated
through, stirring constantly. Spread over 1 side of each bread slice. Cut
each bread slice into 3 equal pieces. Arrange on a baking sheet. Bake at
250 degrees for 1 hour. Remove to a wire rack to cool. Store in an
airtight container.

Yield: 6 dozen

Cinnamon Almond Biscotti

³/₄ cup chopped almonds
¹/₂ cup (1 stick) unsalted butter, softened
³/₄ cup sugar
2 eggs
1 teaspoon vanilla extract
1 tablespoon brandy or Cognac (optional)
2 cups plus 2 tablespoons flour
1¹/₂ teaspoons baking powder
¹/₂ teaspoon cinnamon
¹/₄ teaspoon freshly grated nutmeg (optional)
¹/₄ teaspoon salt

Spread the almonds evenly in a baking pan. Bake at 350 degrees for 8 to 10 minutes or until lightly toasted. Let stand until cool.

Cream the butter and sugar in a mixing bowl until light and fluffy. Add the eggs and mix well. Beat in the vanilla and brandy. Sift the flour, baking powder, cinnamon, nutmeg and salt into a bowl. Stir in the toasted almonds. Add to the butter mixture and stir just until blended.

Shape the dough into two 1¹/₂×12-inch logs on a lightly floured surface. Place on a greased baking sheet 4 inches apart. Flatten the tops slightly. Bake for 30 minutes or until light brown. Place on a cutting board and let stand for 10 minutes. Cut diagonally into ¹/₂-inch-thick slices. Arrange the slices cut side down on the baking sheet. Bake for 10 minutes and turn. Bake for an additional 10 minutes or until light brown. Remove to a wire rack to cool. Store in an airtight container.

Yield: 2¹/₂ dozen

When rain spoiled an outdoor party Frederic held for Evelyn at their Essex farm, he was determined never to have weather interfere with another party. He immediately began plans for the Bothways Hunting Lodge to fit their entertainment needs.

The Bartletts
maintained a weekend
house near the
Everglades in Davie,
Florida, called
Nymphenglade.

Apricot Sticks

$^1/_2$ cup (1 stick) butter
$^1/_2$ cup sugar
1   teaspoon grated lemon zest
2   egg yolks
1   cup flour
$^1/_2$ teaspoon salt
$^1/_4$ teaspoon baking soda
1$^1/_2$ cups apricot jam
2   egg whites
$^1/_4$ cup sugar
$^1/_2$ cup chopped nuts
     Confectioners' sugar

Cream the butter, $^1/_2$ cup sugar and lemon zest in a mixing bowl until light and fluffy. Add the egg yolks 1 at a time, mixing well after each addition. Add the flour, salt and baking soda and mix well. Spread over the bottom of a greased 9×13-inch baking pan.

Spread the jam evenly over the batter. Beat the egg whites in a bowl until soft peaks form. Add $^1/_4$ cup sugar gradually, beating until stiff peaks form. Fold in the nuts. Spread over the jam.

Bake at 350 degrees for 45 minutes. Let stand until cool. Cut into strips. Sprinkle with confectioners' sugar.

Yield: 4 dozen

Dinner

The staff would have their
main meal at 12:00 noon;
it wasn't called "lunch"
then. The meals were called
"breakfast, dinner, and
supper." Dinner for the
Bartletts and Mr. Birch was
served at 1:00 P.M.

Sponsored by
Auto Nation

The Bamboo Bar adjoining the Shell Museum was an intimate setting for before-dinner cocktails.

Andrew Itkoff

This Pavilion was used by the Bartletts
for afternoon lounging, playing cards,
and entertaining friends. A colorful mural
of a princess on a pink elephant painted
by Frederic served as a backdrop. The
Pavilion overlooks the south pond where the
Spatterdock or Bonnet Lily grows. Bonnet
House was named after the Bonnet Lily.

Dining with the Bartletts in
the courtyard combined a
garden atmosphere with
Mrs. Bartlett's carefully
chosen table setting and
the chef's delectable meal.

Tony Branco ©

Tony Branco ©

Theodore Flagg

Green wine bottle with oranges,
watercolor by Mrs. Bartlett.

John Pearce ©

Main (South) Entrance to Bonnet House with Cowfish
Set off by the obelisks that were a favorite decorative
element of Frederic Bartlett, the gate reveals the
fountain and covered walkway connecting the studio,
house, and a building that now includes a gallery
of Mrs. Bartlett's paintings.

Table of Contents

Sponsored by

Publix Super Market Charities

Herbed Tomato Bruschetta

2   baguettes, cut into ¹/₄-inch slices
1¹/₂ pounds plum tomatoes, seeded, chopped
¹/₃ cup chopped basil
1   tablespoon chopped garlic
1   tablespoon balsamic vinegar
1   tablespoon olive oil
1   tablespoon fresh lemon juice

Arrange the baguette slices on a baking sheet. Lightly toast on both sides under a broiler. Combine the tomatoes, basil, garlic, vinegar, olive oil and lemon juice in a bowl and mix well. Serve the tomato mixture with the toasted bread slices or spooned over the toasted bread slices.

Yield: Variable

Spiced Nuts

2   tablespoons olive oil
¹/₂ teaspoon crushed garlic
¹/₂ teaspoon cumin
¹/₂ teaspoon chili powder
¹/₄ teaspoon cinnamon
¹/₄ teaspoon ground ginger
¹/₄ teaspoon curry powder
¹/₄ teaspoon cayenne pepper
2   cups blanched whole almonds
2   cups pecan halves

Heat the olive oil in a large skillet over medium heat. Stir in the garlic, cumin, chili powder, cinnamon, ginger, curry powder and cayenne pepper. Add the almonds. Cook for 4 minutes, stirring constantly. Add the pecans. Stir until pecans are coated. Spoon evenly over the bottom of a 10×15-inch baking pan. Bake at 325 degrees for 15 minutes, stirring every 5 minutes. Let stand until cool.

Yield: 14 to 16 servings

The Bartletts would usually entertain small groups at dinner and would reciprocate immediately for social engagements with others.

Mushroom Strudel

1/4 cup (1/2 stick) butter, melted	Mushroom Filling
1/2 cup olive oil	1 package béarnaise sauce,
16 sheets frozen phyllo dough	prepared

Combine the butter and olive oil in a small bowl and mix well. Layer 8 sheets of the phyllo dough, brushing each sheet with the olive oil mixture. Spread half of the Mushroom Filling over the layers. Roll the dough tightly as for a jelly roll. Place seam side down on a greased baking sheet. Brush with the olive oil mixture. Repeat with the remaining ingredients. Bake at 350 degrees for 30 minutes or until golden brown. Let stand until cool. Cut into 1-inch thick slices. Serve with the béarnaise sauce. Baked strudels may be refrigerated and warmed prior to slicing.

Yield: 10 servings

Mushroom Filling

1 1/2 pounds fresh mushrooms	1/4 teaspoon thyme
Grated zest of 1 lemon	Salt and black pepper to taste
Juice of 1 lemon	1 garlic clove
1 medium onion, cut into	1/2 teaspoon cayenne pepper
large pieces	2 tablespoons olive oil
1/2 cup chopped fresh parsley	2 egg whites
2 celery ribs	1/2 cup sour cream

Remove the stems from the mushrooms. Process the mushroom stems and lemon zest with 1 tablespoon of the lemon juice in a food processor fitted with a steel blade until finely minced. Spoon into a bowl and set aside. Cut the mushroom caps into 1/4-inch thick slices. Sprinkle with the remaining lemon juice. Process the onion, parsley, celery, thyme, salt, black pepper, garlic and cayenne pepper in the food processor until finely minced. Heat the olive oil in a skillet. Add the onion mixture. Sauté until onions are tender. Add the minced mushroom stems and the sliced mushroom caps. Sauté until liquid has evaporated. Remove from the heat. Beat the egg whites in a bowl until soft peaks form. Fold in the sour cream and mushroom mixture.

Italian Strata

1   (8-count) can crescent rolls
4   ounces baked ham, sliced
4   ounces Swiss cheese, sliced
4   ounces Genoa salami, sliced
4   ounces Provolone cheese, sliced
4   ounces pepperoni, sliced
1   (7-ounce) jar roasted red bell peppers, drained
3   eggs, beaten
1   (8-count) can crescent rolls

Unroll 1 package crescent rolls; do not separate. Place over the bottom of a greased 9×13-inch baking pan, pressing the perforations to seal. Layer the ham, Swiss cheese, salami, Provolone cheese, pepperoni and bell peppers over the crescent roll dough.

Pour the eggs over the layers. Unroll 1 package crescent rolls; do not separate. Place over the layers, stretching gently to cover and sealing to the edges.

Bake, covered, at 350 degrees for 30 minutes. Remove the cover. Bake for an additional 30 minutes, replacing the cover if top becomes too brown. Let stand for 30 minutes. Cut into pieces and place on paper towels to drain.

Yield: 50 to 60 servings

Dinner

Really Yummy Oysters Rockefeller Casserole

1 pint shucked oysters	$^1/_4$ cup light cream
2 (10-ounce) packages frozen chopped spinach, thawed	$^1/_2$ cup grated Parmesan cheese
	Salt and pepper to taste
$^1/_4$ cup ($^1/_2$ stick) butter	Freshly grated nutmeg
$^1/_4$ cup flour	2 tablespoons grated Parmesan cheese
2 cups milk	
2 egg yolks	2 baguettes, thickly sliced

Arrange the undrained oysters in a greased 9×13-inch baking dish. Drain the spinach, pressing out the excess moisture. Spread the spinach evenly over the oysters. Heat the butter in a saucepan over low heat until melted. Stir in the flour. Cook for 3 to 5 minutes, stirring constantly. Add the milk, stirring constantly. Cook until sauce has thickened, stirring constantly. Beat the egg yolks with the cream in a bowl. Stir a small amount of the hot mixture into the beaten eggs; stir the eggs into the hot mixture. Whisk in $^1/_2$ cup cheese. Stir until smooth. Season with salt and pepper. Pour over the spinach. Sprinkle nutmeg and 2 tablespoons cheese over the top. Bake at 325 degrees for 20 to 25 minutes or until lightly browned. Serve with the baguette slices.

Yield: 26 to 30 servings

Barbecue Shrimp

$^1/_2$ cup (1 stick) butter	$^1/_2$ cup liquid cayenne pepper
1 (12-ounce) bottle Italian dressing	3 pounds (21- to 25-count) unpeeled shrimp

Combine the butter, dressing and cayenne pepper in a large saucepan. Bring to a simmer. Simmer for 5 minutes. Add the shrimp. Cook for 4 to 5 minutes or until shrimp turn pink. Serve in a soup plate.

Yield: 8 to 10 servings

Dinner
Rosemary Focaccia Loaves

5¹/₂ cups unbleached white flour
2   teaspoons salt
2   envelopes dry yeast
¹/₂ cup warm (110-degrees) water
1   tablespoon sugar
¹/₂ cup extra-virgin olive oil
2   tablespoons chopped fresh rosemary
1¹/₂ cups warm (110-degrees) water
      Extra-virgin olive oil for brushing bread

Combine the flour and salt in a bowl. Combine the yeast, ¹/₂ cup warm water and sugar in a large bowl. Let stand for 10 minutes or until foamy. Add ¹/₂ cup olive oil, rosemary and 1¹/₂ cups warm water and mix well. Add 5 cups of the flour mixture 1 cup at a time, mixing well after each addition. Add the remaining flour mixture gradually, mixing well after each addition.

Knead the dough on a greased and floured surface for 5 to 10 minutes or until smooth and elastic. Place in a greased bowl, turning to coat the surface. Let rise, covered, in a warm place for 1¹/₂ hours or until doubled in bulk.

Divide dough into 2 equal portions. Grease two 5×9-inch loaf pans. Press each portion into a prepared loaf pan. Let rise, covered, in a warm place for 30 minutes. Preheat the oven to 450 degrees. Dimple the dough with fingertips. Brush both loaves with olive oil. Reduce the oven temperature to 375 degrees. Bake for 20 to 25 minutes. Remove from the pans. Cool on a wire rack.

Yield: 2 loaves

Mary Wilcox, a close friend of the Bartletts and frequent dinner guest at Bonnet House, says that table conversation was always stimulating. Houseguests were very prominent people, and there was always someone different and exciting.

Dinner

Gruyère Cheese Bread

1	cup water	1	cup flour
6	tablespoons butter	4	eggs
1	teaspoon salt	1	cup finely chopped Gruyère
1/8	teaspoon pepper		cheese

Combine the water, butter, salt and pepper in a saucepan. Bring to a boil.
Add the flour all at once. Cook until mixture forms a ball and leaves the
side of the pan, stirring constantly. Remove from the heat. Beat in the
eggs 1 at a time. Set aside 2 tablespoons of the cheese. Stir the remaining
cheese into the dough. Arrange rounded tablespoonfuls of the dough in
a circle on a greased baking sheet, leaving 2$^{1}/_{2}$ inches in the center.
Sprinkle the reserved cheese over the top. Bake at 425 degrees for 40 to
45 minutes or until puffed and golden brown.

Yield: 6 to 8 servings

Asparagus with Roasted Red Pepper Coulis

3	large red bell peppers, roasted, peeled, seeded (see page 123)	1/2	jalapeño chile, chopped
		1/4	cup red wine vinegar
			Salt to taste
1/4	cup olive oil	18	to 24 asparagus spears, trimmed
3	shallots, sliced		
1	large garlic clove, sliced		

Purée the bell peppers in a blender or food processor. Heat the olive oil
in a skillet until hot. Add the shallots, garlic and jalapeño chile. Cook for
5 minutes or until tender; do not brown. Add to the bell pepper purée.
Add the vinegar to the skillet. Boil for 30 seconds, stirring constantly.
Stir into the bell pepper mixture. Season the coulis with salt. Boil the
asparagus in enough water to cover in a saucepan. Cook just until tender.
Drain and place in a large bowl of ice water. Drain and pat dry. Place a
small amount of the coulis on a plate. Place 3 or 4 asparagus spears over
the coulis. Repeat with the remaining coulis and asparagus.

Yield: 4 to 8 servings

Dinner

Red as a Beet Salad

1   (16-ounce) can beets
1   tablespoon unflavored gelatin
$^1/_4$ cup sugar
$^1/_2$ teaspoon salt
$^1/_2$ cup cider vinegar
2   tablespoons prepared red horseradish
2   tablespoons finely chopped onion
$^1/_2$ cup finely chopped celery
     Sour Cream Dressing

Drain and chop the beets, reserving the juice. Soften the gelatin in $^1/_4$ cup of the reserved beet juice. Add enough water to the remaining beet juice to measure $^1/_2$ cup. Pour into a saucepan. Cook until heated through. Add the softened gelatin, stirring until dissolved. Combine the gelatin mixture, beets, sugar, salt, vinegar, horseradish, onion and celery in a bowl and mix well. Pour into a greased mold. Chill, covered, until firm. Unmold onto a serving plate. Serve with Sour Cream Dressing.

Yield: 4 to 6 servings

Sour Cream Dressing

$^1/_2$ cup sour cream
$^1/_2$ cup mayonnaise
2   tablespoons prepared horseradish

Combine the sour cream, mayonnaise and horseradish in a bowl and mix well.

Frederic Bartlett built the Shell Museum, Orchid House, and Bamboo Bar at Bonnet House as a surprise gift for Evelyn. Luncheon and dinner guests were invited to admire the shells, view the orchids, and be served cocktails and hors d'oeuvre in the Bamboo Bar. The featured drink was the Rangpur Lime Cocktail.

Dinner
Bleu Cheese Apple Salad

1   Red Delicious apple
1   Granny Smith apple
     Watercress
2   to 3 tablespoons crumbled bleu cheese
3   to 4 walnuts, chopped
     Mustard Dressing

Cut the apples into very thin slices. Divide the watercress among 4 serving plates. Arrange the apples over the watercress in a circular pattern, alternating the red and green slices. Sprinkle the bleu cheese and walnuts over the apples. Drizzle Mustard Dressing over the salad.

Yield: 4 servings

Mustard Dressing

2   tablespoons Dijon mustard
3   tablespoons red wine vinegar
7   tablespoons walnut oil
4$\frac{1}{2}$ teaspoons minced parsley or basil
        Salt and pepper to taste

Whisk the mustard and vinegar together in a bowl. Add the walnut oil in a steady stream, whisking constantly. Stir in the parsley, salt and pepper.

Dinner

Bok Choy Salad

¹/₂ cup (1 stick) butter
2 packages oriental-flavor ramen noodles
1 bunch bok choy, rinsed, sliced
6 green onions, sliced
¹/₂ cup sunflower seed kernels
    Oil and Vinegar Dressing

Place the butter in a 10×15-inch baking pan. Place the pan in a 350-degree oven. Heat until butter is melted. Break the noodles into small pieces. Stir into the butter and spread evenly across the pan. Sprinkle the seasoning packages over the noodles. Bake for 8 minutes.

Combine the noodles, bok choy, green onions and sunflower seed kernels in a large bowl and mix well. Pour Oil and Vinegar Dressing over the salad and toss to combine. You may add bite-size pieces of chicken, beef or pork for a main-dish salad.

Yield: 8 servings

Oil and Vinegar Dressing

¹/₂ cup sugar
¹/₂ cup vegetable oil
¹/₄ cup cider vinegar
1 tablespoon soy sauce

Combine the sugar, oil, vinegar and soy sauce in a small saucepan. Bring to a boil. Let stand until cool.

Whether dining alone or with guests, Evelyn would select a different combination of china and linen for each meal. Her collection of china and the handmade set of dishes made by her daughter Evie offered a variety of color, design, and mood for each table setting.

Beef Tenderloin with Peppercorns

People who dined at
Bonnet House could
discern the menu when
they saw the table
setting. The ceramic
birds centerpiece meant
fowl; ceramic fish on
the table meant fish.
Evelyn sometimes
used fresh flowers
from her garden on
the table, but most
often she used her
ceramic decorations.

1   (5- to 6-pound) beef tenderloin
3   tablespoons Dijon mustard
1   tablespoon dried sage
4½ teaspoons green peppercorns, drained
4½ teaspoons whole black peppercorns, ground
4½ teaspoons whole white peppercorns, ground
2   tablespoons butter, softened

Cut the tenderloin lengthwise to within ½ inch of the edge. Open the tenderloin and press flat. Spread the top with the mustard. Sprinkle with the sage, green peppercorns, 1½ teaspoons of the ground black peppercorns and 1½ teaspoons of the ground white peppercorns.

Fold the tenderloin in half lengthwise. Tie with heavy string at 3-inch intervals. Spread the butter over the tenderloin. Sprinkle with the remaining ground black peppercorns and remaining ground white peppercorns. Place the tenderloin on a rack in a broiler pan.

Bake the tenderloin in a preheated 425-degree oven for 30 to 45 minutes or to 135 degrees on a meat thermometer for rare or 150 degrees on a meat thermometer for medium. Let stand for 10 minutes. Cut into slices.

Yield: 10 to 12 servings

Slow-Cooked Brisket

1	(5-pound) beef brisket		1 1/2	teaspoons allspice
2	tablespoons vegetable oil		1/4	cup molasses
2	teaspoons dry mustard		1/4	cup red wine vinegar
2	teaspoons sage		1/2	cup ketchup
2	teaspoons oregano		2	tablespoons tomato paste
1	teaspoon red pepper flakes		1	cup water
1/2	teaspoon cayenne pepper		1	teaspoon salt
4	garlic cloves, minced		1	teaspoon black pepper
2	teaspoons ginger			

Place the brisket in a slow-cooker. Combine the oil, dry mustard, sage, oregano, red pepper flakes, cayenne pepper, garlic, ginger, allspice, molasses, vinegar, ketchup, tomato paste, water, salt and black pepper in a bowl and mix well. Pour over the brisket. Cook on Low for 8 to 10 hours or until brisket can be pulled apart with a fork.

Yield: 12 servings

Caribbean Flank Steak

2	pounds flank steak		2	garlic cloves, minced
1/3	cup fresh lime juice		1/2	teaspoon freshly ground
1/4	cup olive oil			pepper
1/4	cup molasses			Lime slices or wedges
2	tablespoons Dijon mustard			for garnish
1	teaspoon grated lime zest			

Place the steak in a shallow dish. Combine the lime juice, olive oil, molasses, mustard, lime zest, garlic and pepper in a bowl and mix well. Pour over the steak. Marinate, covered, in the refrigerator for 2 hours, turning frequently; drain. Place the steak on a rack in a broiler pan. Broil until done to taste. You may grill the steak. Cut into thin slices on the bias.

Yield: 8 to 10 servings

Dinner
Steak Tournedos

1½	pounds flank steak	1	(4-ounce) container French-style cream cheese with garlic and herbs
½	cup dry red wine		
	Meat tenderizer		
8	ounces bacon slices	2	tablespoons chopped parsley
1	teaspoon minced garlic		Prepared béarnaise sauce
¼	teaspoon pepper		

Pound the steak into ¼-inch thickness and place in a shallow dish. Pour the wine over the steak. Chill, covered, for 3 hours. Use the meat tenderizer following the package directions. Cook the bacon in a skillet until done but not crisp. Remove from the skillet and place on paper towels to drain. Sprinkle the steak with the garlic and pepper. Spread the cream cheese over the steak. Arrange the cooked bacon over the cream cheese. Sprinkle the parsley over the bacon. Roll as for a jelly roll, starting at the narrow end. Secure with skewers at 1-inch intervals. Place on a grill over medium-hot coals. Grill for 15 minutes, turning once, for rare. Cut into slices. Serve with the béarnaise sauce.

Yield: 6 to 8 servings

Sweet-and-Sour Short Ribs

½	cup flour	2	tablespoons vinegar
2	teaspoons salt	2	tablespoons Worcestershire sauce
	Pepper to taste		
5	pounds short ribs	¼	cup soy sauce
2	cups sliced onions	½	cup sugar
¾	cup ketchup	¾	cup water

Mix the flour, salt and pepper in a shallow dish. Dredge the short ribs in the flour mixture, coating on all sides. Arrange in a deep baking pan. Arrange the onions over the ribs. Combine the ketchup, vinegar, Worcestershire sauce, soy sauce, sugar and water in a bowl and mix well. Pour over the onions. Bake, covered, at 300 degrees for 2½ hours. Remove the cover and bake for an additional 30 minutes. Place the ribs on a serving platter. Skim the fat from the sauce. Serve the sauce with the ribs.

Yield: 6 to 8 servings

Veal Piccata

2   tablespoons flour
1/2   teaspoon salt
1/4   teaspoon pepper
1   pound veal scaloppine
1/2   cup (1 stick) butter
1/4   cup dry white wine
1   lemon, sliced
1/4   cup chopped parsley
     Wine Sauce

Combine the flour, salt and pepper in a shallow dish and mix well. Coat the veal lightly with the flour mixture. Heat the butter in a skillet over medium heat until melted. Add the veal and sauté. Add the wine, lemon slices and parsley. Simmer for 10 minutes. Serve with Wine Sauce.

Yields: 4 to 6 servings

Wine Sauce

1   egg yolk
1/4   cup dry white wine
1   tablespoon butter

Combine the egg yolk and wine in a bowl and mix well. Heat the butter in a skillet over low heat until melted. Stir in the wine mixture. Cook over low heat for 2 to 4 minutes or until thickened, stirring constantly.

Each morning, when she was in Florida, Evelyn Bartlett would confer with the cook to plan the day's menu. Only the freshest of food was used. Fresh produce from local grocers and farmers was purchased to supplement shipments from the Massachusetts farm.

73

Hors d'oeuvre served
at Bonnet House were
quite simple: cherry
tomatoes stuffed with
cheese, endive leaves
with a special dip,
homemade turkey liver
pâté, or caramelized
bacon. Evelyn also
loved roasted pecans.

Dinner

Roast Pork with Gingered Fruit Sauce

1	(3-pound) boneless pork loin
1	large onion, chopped
2	garlic cloves, crushed
2	tablespoons vegetable oil
$1/2$	cup soy sauce
1	tablespoon brown sugar
1	teaspoon curry powder
1	teaspoon pepper
1	teaspoon oregano (optional)
	Gingered Fruit Sauce

Place the pork in a large bowl. Combine the onion, garlic, oil, soy sauce, brown sugar, curry powder, pepper and oregano in a small bowl and mix well. Pour over the pork. Marinate, covered, in the refrigerator for 4 hours, turning occasionally. Drain and place in a shallow roasting pan. Roast at 375 degrees for $1^1/2$ hours or to 145 degrees on a meat thermometer. Serve with Gingered Fruit Sauce.

Yield: 10 to 12 servings

Gingered Fruit Sauce

1	cup orange marmalade
2	tablespoons orange juice
2	tablespoons lemon juice
$1^1/2$	teaspoons prepared horseradish
1	small piece fresh gingerroot, peeled, crushed
1	teaspoon dry mustard

Process the marmalade, orange juice and lemon juice in a blender or food processor until combined. Spoon into a bowl. Add the horseradish, gingerroot and dry mustard and mix well. May be stored in the refrigerator for several weeks.

German-Style Pork Tenderloin

3	(15-ounce) cans sauerkraut, drained		Salt and pepper
6	Granny Smith apples, sliced	1	cup meat stock
1/2	cup packed brown sugar	1/2	cup dry white wine (optional)
4	(1-pound) pork tenderloins		

Combine the sauerkraut, apples and brown sugar in a bowl and mix well. Spread half over the bottom of a 9×13-inch baking dish. Sprinkle the pork with salt and pepper. Arrange over the sauerkraut mixture. Spread the remaining sauerkraut mixture over the pork. Pour the stock and wine over the layers. Bake, covered, at 350 degrees for 1 hour.

Yield: 8 servings

Maple Barbecued Pork Ribs

1	cup maple syrup	4	garlic cloves, pressed
1	cup ketchup	1/2	teaspoon salt
1	cup finely chopped onion	1/2	teaspoon hot sauce
1/4	cup packed light brown sugar	3	pounds country-style pork ribs
1/4	cup apple cider vinegar		
1/2	cup water	3	to 4 1/2 teaspoons lemon pepper
2	tablespoons olive oil		
2	tablespoons Worcestershire sauce		

Combine the maple syrup, ketchup, onion, brown sugar, vinegar, water, olive oil, Worcestershire sauce, garlic, salt and hot sauce in a saucepan and mix well. Bring to a boil. Reduce the heat. Simmer for 20 minutes. Let stand until cool. Reserve 1 cup of the sauce. Rub the ribs with lemon pepper. Place on a grill over medium-hot coals. Grill, covered, for 25 to 30 minutes. Brush with the remaining sauce. Grill for an additional 10 to 15 minutes or until cooked through. Serve with the reserved sauce. You may bake the pork ribs, loosely covered, at 350 degrees for 25 to 35 minutes on each side and then brush with the sauce and bake, uncovered, for an additional 15 minutes.

Yield: 4 to 6 servings

Dinner

Basil Lemon Roast Chicken with New Potatoes

1	(4-pound) roasting chicken	2	pounds new potatoes
6	garlic cloves, cut into slivers	1/2	cup olive oil
1	small bunch basil	3	garlic cloves, minced
2	lemons, cut into halves		Black peppercorns

Place the chicken in a foil-lined roasting pan. Place garlic slivers, basil and 2 lemon halves in the cavity. Squeeze the juice from the remaining 2 lemon halves over the chicken. Rub the chicken with the lemon halves. Place in the chicken cavity. Truss the chicken. Arrange the potatoes around the chicken. Drizzle the olive oil over the chicken and potatoes. Sprinkle the minced garlic over the potatoes. Grind the pepper over the chicken and potatoes. Bake at 375 degrees for 1 hour or until juices run clear when leg is pierced. Remove from the oven. Let chicken stand for 10 to 15 minutes.

Yield: 4 to 6 servings

Forty Cloves of Garlic Chicken

1	(2 1/2-pound) chicken	4	to 6 new potatoes, cut into
1/2	teaspoon thyme		halves
1/2	teaspoon rosemary	8	carrots, peeled, cut into
	Salt and pepper		2-inch pieces
40	unpeeled garlic cloves	1/2	cup dry white wine

Rinse the chicken and pat the cavity and outside dry. Sprinkle with the thyme, rosemary, salt and pepper. Place in a roasting pan. Arrange the garlic, potatoes and carrots around the chicken. Bake at 350 degrees for 20 minutes. Pour the wine over the chicken and vegetables. Bake for 2 hours or until chicken is cooked through, basting every 20 minutes with pan drippings. Cut into pieces. Arrange the chicken pieces, garlic, potatoes and carrots on a serving platter. Pour the pan juices over the chicken and vegetables. You may peel the garlic before placing on the platter.

Yield: 4 to 6 servings

Dinner

Apple Curried Chicken Breasts

1 tablespoon curry powder
2 tablespoons olive oil
8 boneless skinless chicken breast halves
 Salt and freshly ground pepper
1 tablespoon butter
2 garlic cloves, minced
2 shallots, minced
2 teaspoons minced fresh gingerroot
1/2 cup white wine
1/2 cup apple cider or apple juice
1 Gala or Granny Smith apple, chopped
1 cup light cream or evaporated milk

Heat the curry powder in a small skillet over medium-high heat for 2 minutes or until aromatic. Set aside.

Heat the olive oil in a large skillet over medium-high heat. Season the chicken with salt and pepper. Sear the chicken on both sides in the hot oil. Remove and set aside. Add the butter to the skillet. Add the garlic and shallots and cook until golden brown, stirring constantly. Stir in the gingerroot, wine and apple cider. Bring to a boil.

Add the apple to the skillet and cook for 1 to 2 minutes. Reduce the heat to medium. Stir in the toasted curry powder and cream. Place the chicken breasts in the sauce. Simmer for 10 to 15 minutes or until chicken is cooked through, stirring frequently. Serve over basmati rice.

Yield: 6 to 8 servings

Wine was served at the main meal of the day, and there were always wonderful desserts.

Chicken with Champagne Sauce

4	boneless skinless chicken breast halves	$^3/_4$	cup Champagne
2	tablespoons butter	$^1/_2$	cup heavy cream
$^1/_2$	cup chopped shallots	$^1/_4$	teaspoon salt
		1	tablespoon butter

Pound the chicken into $^1/_2$-inch thickness between sheets of plastic wrap. Heat 2 tablespoons butter in a skillet until melted. Add the chicken. Sauté for 3 to 4 minutes on each side or until golden. Remove to a platter and keep warm.

Add the shallots to the butter and cook until tender. Stir in the Champagne. Cook over high heat until reduced by half. Stir in the cream and salt. Cook until sauce thickens slightly, stirring frequently; do not boil. Whisk in 1 tablespoon butter. Place 1 chicken breast on each dinner plate. Spoon the sauce over the chicken.

Yield: 4 servings

Chicken Rosemary in Mushroom Sauce

2	tablespoons butter	$^1/_2$	cup white wine
6	boneless skinless chicken breast halves	$^1/_2$	teaspoon basil
1	(10-ounce) can cream of mushroom soup	$^1/_2$	teaspoon rosemary
8	ounces fresh mushrooms, sliced	$^1/_2$	cup thinly sliced onion

Heat the butter in a large skillet until melted. Add the chicken. Cook until browned on both sides. Place in a greased baking dish. Combine the soup, mushrooms, wine, basil, rosemary and onion in a bowl and mix well. Spoon over the chicken. Cook, covered, at 350 degrees for 1 hour.

Yield: 6 servings

Plum Wonderful Chicken

2   tablespoons olive oil or vegetable oil
2 1/2 pounds boneless skinless chicken breast halves
1/4 cup finely chopped onion
1   garlic clove, minced
1   teaspoon grated fresh gingerroot
1/3 cup plum sauce
1/4 cup frozen lemonade concentrate
1/4 cup chili sauce
1   tablespoon lemon juice
1   teaspoon dry mustard

Heat the olive oil in a large skillet over medium-high heat. Cook the chicken in the hot olive oil over medium heat for 10 minutes or until brown on both sides. Place the chicken in a 3-quart baking dish. Discard the pan drippings, reserving 1 tablespoon. Add the onion, garlic and gingerroot to the reserved drippings. Cook until onion is tender.

Combine the plum sauce, lemonade concentrate, chili sauce, lemon juice and dry mustard in a bowl and mix well. Stir into the onion mixture. Bring to a boil. Reduce the heat. Simmer, covered, for 5 minutes. Spoon over the chicken. Bake at 350 degrees for 40 to 45 minutes or until chicken is cooked through, basting with the sauce.

Yield: 6 servings

The staff would have their main meal at 12:00 noon; it wasn't called "lunch" then. The meals were called "breakfast, dinner, and supper." Dinner for the Bartletts and Mr. Birch was served at 1:00 P.M.

Scaloppine di Pollo

4 boneless skinless chicken breast halves	1/2 teaspoon crushed basil
1 egg, beaten	1/4 cup olive oil
1 tablespoon water	2 garlic cloves, crushed
1/2 cup Italian-flavored bread crumbs	1/4 cup dry sherry or white wine
	1 lemon, thinly sliced
	1 tablespoon capers (optional)

Pound the chicken until thin between sheets of plastic wrap. Beat the egg with the water in a shallow dish. Combine the bread crumbs and basil in a separate shallow dish. Heat the olive oil with the garlic in a large skillet over medium heat. Remove the garlic. Dip a chicken breast into the egg mixture. Dredge in the bread crumb mixture to coat. Place in the hot oil. Repeat with the remaining chicken breasts. Cook the chicken for 3 minutes on each side. Remove to a platter and keep warm. Pour the sherry into the pan and scrape the bottom of the skillet with a wooden spoon to remove any browned bits. Spoon over the chicken. Arrange the lemon slices and capers over the top.

Yield: 2 to 4 servings

Magic Turkey Breast

1 (4- to 6-pound) turkey breast	1 teaspoon thyme
3 tablespoons lemon pepper	1 teaspoon crushed rosemary
3 tablespoons garlic powder	1 tablespoon flour

Remove and discard the skin from the turkey. Pat the turkey dry. Spray with butter-flavor cooking spray. Combine the lemon pepper, garlic powder, thyme and rosemary in a bowl and mix well. Sprinkle over the turkey, coating thoroughly. Place a 14×20-inch oven cooking bag in a 9×13-inch baking pan. Add the flour to the bag. Twist the end and shake to coat the inside of the bag. Place the turkey in the bag and close with the twist tie provided. Cut six 1/2-inch slits in the top of the bag. Bake at 350 degrees for 15 to 19 minutes per pound or until cooked through. Remove turkey from the bag. Cut into slices.

Yield: 6 to 8 servings

Dinner

Grouper Sautéed with Tomatoes, Pine Nuts and Goat Cheese

1	tablespoon vegetable oil
1/4	cup flour
4	(6- to 8-ounce) grouper fillets
4	garlic cloves, minced
1/4	cup chopped fresh basil
1/4	cup pine nuts, toasted
4	plum tomatoes, chopped
1/4	cup dry sherry
	Juice of 1 lemon
	Salt and freshly ground black pepper to taste
1/2	cup crumbled goat cheese, such as Montrachet
6	scallions, cut into 1/4-inch pieces

Heat the oil in a large skillet over medium-high heat. Place the flour in a shallow dish. Dip the grouper in the flour to coat lightly. Cook in the hot oil for 5 minutes on each side or until golden brown. Remove to a platter and keep warm.

Add the garlic to the hot oil. Reduce the heat. Cook for 1 minute, stirring constantly. Add the basil, pine nuts, tomatoes, sherry and lemon juice. Cook over high heat for 2 minutes. Add the grouper to the sauce. Season with salt and pepper. Cook until heated through.

Place 1 grouper fillet on each of 4 plates. Spoon the tomato mixture evenly over the grouper. Sprinkle the cheese and scallions over the top.

Yield: 4 servings

Supper was a light meal—usually soup, a cheese soufflé, or a salad.

Dinner

Grilled Salmon

4   salmon fillets or steaks
1/4 cup dry vermouth
1/2 cup vegetable oil
2   tablespoons fresh lemon juice
3/4 teaspoon salt
1/8 teaspoon pepper
1/2 teaspoon thyme
1/2 teaspoon marjoram
1/4 teaspoon sage
1   tablespoon chopped fresh parsley
     Cucumber Sauce

Arrange the salmon in a single layer in a nonreactive shallow dish. Combine the vermouth, oil, lemon juice, salt, pepper, thyme, marjoram, sage and parsley in a bowl and mix well. Pour over the salmon. Marinate, covered, in the refrigerator, for 1 hour, turning once.

Drain the salmon. Place on a grill over hot coals. Grill until salmon flakes easily. Serve with Cucumber Sauce.

Yield: 4 servings

Cucumber Sauce

2 1/3 cups light sour cream
1/2 teaspoon finely chopped onion
1   large cucumber, seeded, chopped
     Salt and pepper to taste
4 1/2 teaspoons fresh lemon juice
     Fresh or dried dill to taste

Combine the sour cream, onion, cucumber, salt, pepper, lemon juice and dill in a bowl and mix well. Chill, covered, before serving.

Dinner

Drunken Swordfish

1   to 1¹/2 pounds (¹/4- to ¹/2-inch thick) swordfish steaks
¹/4   cup tequila
      Juice of 2 limes
1   tablespoon chopped cilantro
1   tablespoon minced fresh herbs, such as parsley, tarragon,
      basil and mint
      Salt and pepper to taste
      Barbecue Sauce
      Fresh herbs for garnish

Arrange the swordfish in a single layer in a nonreactive shallow dish. Combine the tequila, lime juice, cilantro, fresh herbs, salt and pepper in a bowl and mix well. Pour over the swordfish. Marinate, covered, in the refrigerator for 2 hours, turning once.

Drain the swordfish. Place on a grill over hot coals. Grill for 1 to 2 minutes on each side. Serve with Barbecue Sauce. Garnish with fresh herbs.

Yield: 4 servings

Barbecue Sauce

¹/2   cup hot sauce
¹/4   cup honey
1   tablespoon Tabasco sauce
3   tablespoons butter, melted
1   tablespoon minced garlic
1   tablespoon white vinegar
¹/4   teaspoon celery salt

Combine the hot sauce, honey, Tabasco sauce, butter, garlic, vinegar and salt in a bowl and mix well.

Irene Hart, who lived on the property as a child, recalls, "Mrs. Bartlett had a kind smile. She would chat or converse with us as she passed by. When she went away, she would bring home gifts for us children."

Dinner

Shrimp in Irish Whiskey and Cream

1¹/₂ tablespoons clarified butter
  (see Editor's note)
3   tablespoons minced shallots
1¹/₂ pounds shrimp, peeled,
  deveined

3   tablespoons Irish whiskey
¹/₂ cup heavy cream
Salt and pepper to taste
Chopped parsley for garnish
  (optional)

Heat the butter in a medium skillet over medium heat until melted.
Add the shallots and shrimp and sauté until the shrimp turn pink. Add
the whiskey and heat briefly. Ignite the liquid, shaking the pan until the
flames subside. Stir in the cream. Cook for 15 minutes or until liquid is
reduced by half, stirring occasionally. Season with salt and pepper. Spoon
into a serving bowl. Garnish with parsley.

Yield: 4 servings

Editor's Note: To make clarified butter, heat the butter in a heavy saucepan
over low heat until melted. Remove from the heat and let stand for
5 minutes or longer. Skim off the foam. The clear liquid is the clarified
butter. Two tablespoons of unsalted butter will yield approximately
1¹/₂ tablespoons of clarified butter.

Roasted Beets

1   beet per serving, scrubbed,
  rinsed
  Salt and pepper to taste

Sour cream
Shredded carrot for garnish
Fresh dill sprigs for garnish

Cut off the beet stems leaving ¹/₂ inch. Place in a baking dish. Bake,
covered, at 450 degrees for 1 hour. Slip the skins off the warm beets; to
avoid staining, wear rubber gloves. Cut off the stems and trim the tails.
Sprinkle with salt and pepper. Let cool. Place each beet on a bed of sour
cream. Garnish with carrot and dill sprigs. Sour cream may be flavored
with lemon juice, dill, curry powder, dry mustard or salt and pepper.

Yield: Variable

Dinner

Bleu Broccoli with Walnuts

1 1/2	pounds fresh broccoli	1/2	cup coarsely chopped
4	ounces creamy bleu cheese		walnuts
1/4	cup heavy cream	1/4	teaspoon freshly ground
2	teaspoons unsalted butter		pepper
1	small garlic clove, minced		

Cut the broccoli into florets, reserving the stems. Cut the stems into
3-inch pieces. Peel and julienne the stem pieces. Steam the broccoli until
tender-crisp; drain. Place in a large bowl of ice water. Combine the bleu
cheese and cream in a small bowl and mix until almost smooth.

Heat the butter in a large saucepan until melted. Add the garlic and
walnuts. Cook for 10 minutes or until light brown, stirring constantly.
Fold the broccoli into the walnut mixture. Stir in the bleu cheese
mixture. Sprinkle with the pepper. Toss until warmed through.

Yield: 4 to 6 servings

Zesty Carrots

6	large carrots	1	teaspoon salt
	(about 1 1/4 pounds), peeled,	1/4	teaspoon pepper
	thinly sliced	2	tablespoons butter or
1/2	cup mayonnaise		margarine, melted
2	tablespoons grated onion	1/4	cup dry bread crumbs
2	tablespoons prepared		
	horseradish		

Bring enough water to cover the carrots to a boil in a saucepan. Add the
carrots. Cook, covered, for 6 to 8 minutes. Drain, reserving 1/4 cup of the
liquid. Place the carrots in a baking dish. Combine the reserved liquid,
mayonnaise, onion, horseradish, salt and pepper in a bowl and mix well.
Pour over the carrots. Combine the butter and bread crumbs in a bowl
and mix well. Sprinkle over the top. Bake at 375 degrees for 15 minutes.

Yield: 6 servings

"A special time was
when we would have
tea and cookies with
Mrs. Bartlett. She
would invite us upstairs
for cookies and to
watch home movies."

—Irene Hart

Vidalia Onion Rice Casserole

$^1/_4$ cup ($^1/_2$ stick) butter
8 large Vidalia onions, cut into quarters
1 cup water
$^1/_2$ cup rice
$^1/_2$ teaspoon salt
1 cup shredded Swiss cheese
$^3/_4$ cup half-and-half

Heat the butter in a skillet until melted. Add the onions and sauté until tender; do not brown. Bring the water to a boil in a saucepan. Add the rice and salt. Simmer, covered, for 5 minutes; drain. Combine the rice, onions and cheese in a bowl and mix well. Stir in the half-and-half. Spoon into a 2-quart baking dish. Bake at 325 degrees for 1 hour.

Yield: 8 to 10 servings

Oven-Fried Garlic Potatoes

1 large baking potato
2 to 3 tablespoons grated Parmesan cheese
2 large garlic cloves, minced
$^1/_4$ teaspoon paprika
$^1/_2$ teaspoon pepper
Dash of salt (optional)
Peanut or vegetable oil

Line a shallow baking dish, large enough to hold the potato wedges in a single layer, with foil. Scrub the potato. Cut lengthwise into 6 or 8 wedges. Combine the cheese, garlic, paprika, pepper and salt in a bowl and mix well. Add enough peanut oil to make of a spreading consistency. Spread over the potato wedges. Place the potato wedges, skin side down, in the prepared dish, adding additional oil if needed. Bake at 375 degrees for 1 hour.

Yield: 2 servings

Dinner

Spaghetti Squash with Brandy Cream Sauce

1   large spaghetti squash (about 2 pounds)
2   cups fresh spinach
1   tablespoon butter or margarine
3   tablespoons minced shallots
1   cup thinly sliced mushrooms
1   cup heavy cream
2   tablespoons brandy
1   cup shredded Monterey Jack cheese
$^1/_2$ teaspoon pepper

Pierce the squash 6 to 8 times with a fork. Place on a layer of paper towels in a microwave. Microwave on High for 15 to 18 minutes or until soft, turning every 5 minutes. Let stand for 5 minutes. Cut in half and discard the seeds. Scoop out the pulp and place in a bowl.

Bring a small amount of water to a boil in a saucepan. Add the spinach. Cook until wilted. Drain and press out the excess moisture. Heat the butter in a skillet until melted. Add the shallots and sauté until tender. Add the mushrooms and sauté for 3 minutes. Add the mushroom mixture to the squash pulp.

Pour the cream and brandy into the skillet. Bring to a boil. Boil for 3 minutes. Stir in the spinach, squash mixture, cheese and pepper. Cook for 1 minute, stirring constantly. You may substitute 5 cups of cooked angel hair pasta for the spaghetti squash.

Yield: 6 servings

"There was such a special feeling at Bonnet House. Everything was nice and you were part of it. It was home and we were treated like it was home."

—Marie Little, cook

Mushroom Risotto

1/4	cup (1/2 stick) butter	6	cups simmering chicken stock
11/2	pounds mushrooms, such as cremini, button and shiitake, thinly sliced	1/4	cup freshly grated Parmigiano-Reggiano cheese
3	tablespoons butter	2	tablespoons chopped fresh flat-leaf parsley for garnish
1	onion, chopped		Freshly grated Parmigiano-Reggiano cheese for garnish
2	cups Italian arborio rice		
1	cup dry white wine		

Heat 1/4 cup butter in a large skillet until melted. Add the mushrooms. Sauté until tender and set aside. Heat 3 tablespoons butter in a Dutch oven or large heavy skillet until melted. Add the onion. Sauté for 2 to 3 minutes or until tender. Stir in the rice. Cook for 1 to 2 minutes or until rice is coated with the butter and onion. Pour in the wine. Cook over medium heat until wine has almost evaporated, stirring constantly. Add 1/2 cup of the stock. Cook for 15 minutes or until stock is almost absorbed, stirring constantly. Repeat with the remaining stock; rice will be tender and firm to the bite. Add the cooked mushrooms and cheese, stirring for 1 to 2 minutes. Garnish with parsley and additional cheese.

Yield: 4 to 8 servings

Spicy Rice

1	cup rice	2/3	cup pimento-stuffed olives, sliced
2	(10-ounce) cans tomatoes with green chiles, chopped	1/2	cup chopped onion
1	cup water	1	cup shredded Monterey Jack cheese
1	teaspoon salt		
1/4	cup vegetable oil		

Combine the rice, tomatoes, water, salt, oil, olives, onion and cheese in a bowl and mix well. Spoon into a greased shallow 2-quart baking dish. Bake, covered, at 350 degrees for 45 minutes. Remove the cover and stir. Bake, uncovered, for an additional 15 minutes or until liquid is absorbed and rice is tender.

Yield: 6 to 8 servings

Perfectly Perfect Chocolate Cake

2	cups sugar	2	eggs
1³/4	cups flour	1	cup milk
³/4	cup baking cocoa	¹/2	cup vegetable oil
1¹/2	teaspoons baking powder	2	teaspoons vanilla extract
1¹/2	teaspoons baking soda	1	cup boiling water
1	teaspoon salt		Perfect Chocolate Frosting

Combine the sugar, flour, baking cocoa, baking powder, baking soda and salt in a mixing bowl and mix well. Add the eggs, milk, oil and vanilla. Beat at medium speed for 2 minutes. Stir in the boiling water; batter will be thin.

Pour into two greased and floured 9-inch round cake pans. Bake at 350 degrees for 30 to 35 minutes or until a wooden pick inserted in the center comes out clean. Cool in the pans for 10 minutes. Remove to a wire rack to cool completely. Spread Perfect Chocolate Frosting between the layers and over the top and side of the cooled cake.

Yield: 10 to 12 servings

Perfect Chocolate Frosting

¹/2	cup (1 stick) butter or margarine, melted	3	cups confectioners' sugar
²/3	cup baking cocoa	¹/3	cup (or more) milk
		1	teaspoon vanilla extract

Combine the butter and baking cocoa in a mixing bowl and mix well. Add the confectioners' sugar and milk alternately, mixing well after each addition. Beat at medium speed until of a spreading consistency. Stir in the vanilla. Beat in additional milk, 1 tablespoon at a time, if needed to make of a thinner consistency.

Evelyn Bartlett's orchid collection was a special part of her life. During her winter visits to Bonnet House she made daily walks to the orchid house to admire the flowers. Fresh cuttings were kept throughout the house and used to decorate the dining table.

Raspberry Fudge Cake

$^1/_4$ cup baking cocoa
1   cup flour
$^3/_4$ teaspoon baking powder
$^1/_4$ teaspoon salt
4   ounces semisweet chocolate
4   ounces unsweetened chocolate
$^3/_4$ cup (1$^1/_2$ sticks) butter
$^3/_4$ cup sugar
$^3/_4$ cup seedless raspberry jam
$^1/_4$ cup cherry liqueur
3   eggs
1   ounce semisweet chocolate
1   tablespoon butter
$^1/_4$ cup seedless raspberry jam
     Freshly whipped cream
     Fresh mint for garnish

Grease a 9-inch springform pan. Dust with baking cocoa. Combine the flour, baking powder and salt in a bowl and mix well. Heat 3 ounces semisweet chocolate, unsweetened chocolate and $^3/_4$ cup butter in a heavy saucepan over low heat until melted, stirring constantly. Whisk the sugar, $^3/_4$ cup jam, liqueur and eggs together in a bowl. Whisk in the flour mixture and chocolate mixture. Pour into the prepared pan. Bake at 350 degrees for 40 to 45 minutes or until set. Cool on a rack for 10 minutes. Remove the side from the pan. Let stand until completely cool.

Heat 1 ounce semisweet chocolate and 1 tablespoon butter in a saucepan until melted, stirring constantly. Cool until slightly thickened. Spread $^1/_4$ cup jam over the cake. Cut the cake into slices. Place 1 slice on each dessert plate. Drizzle with the chocolate sauce. Spoon a dollop of whipped cream on each slice. Garnish with a fresh mint sprig.

Yield: 8 servings

Walnut Tart

1/3   cup butter, softened
1/4   cup sugar
1   (or more) egg yolk
1   cup flour
2   cups coarsely chopped walnuts
1/3   cup butter
2/3   cup packed light brown sugar
1/4   cup dark corn syrup
2   tablespoons heavy cream

Beat 1/3 cup butter and sugar in a bowl until light and fluffy. Beat in the
egg yolk. Beat in the flour; mixture will be crumbly. Add additional egg
yolk if mixture is too dry. Shape into a ball. Press over the bottom and up
the side of a tart pan. Bake at 375 degrees for 12 minutes or until light
brown. Cool on a wire rack.

Spread the walnuts over a baking sheet. Bake at 375 degrees for 5 minutes.
Let stand until cool. Sprinkle over the bottom of the tart crust.

Combine 1/3 cup butter, brown sugar, corn syrup and cream in a heavy
2-quart saucepan and mix well. Bring to a boil over medium heat, stirring
constantly. Boil for 1 minute. Pour over the walnuts.

Bake the tart at 375 degrees for 10 minutes or until bubbly. Place on
a wire rack to cool slightly. Remove tart from the pan. Serve warm with
whipped cream or ice cream.

Yield: 10 to 12 servings

Cheesecake Squares

Evelyn Bartlett
loved animals. In
photographs taken of
her on the property
over a sixty-year
period, she is
invariably holding a
dog or standing with a
pet monkey or a parrot
on her shoulder. At
5 P.M. each day, the
wild monkeys knew
to climb out on a
special tree limb that
reached her upstairs
balcony to receive a
bounty of peanuts
from her hands.

2$^1/_2$ cups graham cracker crumbs (about 18 crackers)
$^1/_2$ cup sugar
$^1/_4$ cup ($^1/_2$ stick) butter, melted
24 ounces cream cheese, softened
5 eggs
1 cup sugar
1$^1/_2$ teaspoons vanilla extract
3 cups sour cream
$^1/_2$ cup sugar
1$^1/_2$ teaspoons vanilla extract

Combine the graham cracker crumbs and $^1/_2$ cup sugar in a bowl and mix well. Add the melted butter and mix well. Press over the bottom of a 9×13-inch baking pan.

Beat the cream cheese in a mixing bowl until fluffy. Add the eggs 1 at a time, mixing well after each addition. Add 1 cup sugar and 1$^1/_2$ teaspoons vanilla and beat until smooth. Spread evenly over the graham cracker layer. Bake at 300 degrees for 1 hour.

Combine the sour cream, $^1/_2$ cup sugar and 1$^1/_2$ teaspoons vanilla in a bowl and mix well. Spread evenly over the top. Bake for an additional 5 minutes. Let stand until cool. Chill, covered, for 8 to 12 hours. Cut into squares.

Yield: 10 to 12 servings

Supper

Supper was a light meal—

usually soup,

a cheese soufflé,

or a salad.

Sponsored by

Devereaux Bruch

The Orchid House displays currently blooming orchids from a collection that has in the past reached over 1,200 plants.

Monkey climbing on
sculpture of Allee Fountain.
An ornate fountain surprises
visitors entering the Allee between the
Lagoon and Lily Pond.

The Haitian Loggia, a breezeway between
the drawing room and dining room,
combines elaborate inlaid shellwork and faux
painting typical of the whimsical,
decorative style created by the Bartletts.

Tony Branco ©

Tony Branco ©

Bonnet House Archives

Silver Palm, Florida Table,
watercolor by Evelyn Bartlett.

Theodore Flagg

Apples with white pitcher, *by Evelyn Bartlett.*

Table of Contents

Sponsored by

Cookbook Steering Committee

Roasted Red Pepper Spread

1 garlic clove
1 tablespoon olive oil
1 tablespoon balsamic vinegar
1 (15-ounce) can garbanzo beans, drained
3 large red bell peppers, roasted, peeled, seeded (see page 123)
1/4 teaspoon salt
1 tablespoon water
1 tablespoon chopped fresh parsley

Chop the garlic finely in a blender or food processor container. Add the olive oil, vinegar and beans and purée. Add the bell peppers, salt, water and parsley and process until smooth. Serve chilled or at room temperature with toasted pita bread triangles or crackers. Refrigerate, tightly covered, for up to 5 days.

Yield: 18 servings

Kahlúa Baked Brie with Pecans

2 cups chopped pecans
1 (12-ounce) wheel of Brie
1/4 cup Kahlúa
2 tablespoons brown sugar

Spread the pecans in a baking sheet. Toast at 350 degrees for 8 to 10 minutes or until light brown. Let stand until cool.

Place the Brie in an ovenproof serving dish. Combine the pecans, Kahlúa and brown sugar in a bowl and mix well. Spread over the cheese. Bake at 350 degrees for 5 minutes. You may place the Brie in a microwave-safe serving dish and microwave for 1 minute. Serve with sliced French bread or crackers.

Yield: 4 to 6 servings

Sesame Chicken Wings

36 chicken drumettes
2 garlic cloves
1 (1-inch cube) fresh gingerroot
1 small onion, cut into quarters
3 tablespoons soy sauce
3 tablespoons fresh lemon juice
2 tablespoons sesame oil
2 tablespoons sugar
2 teaspoons salt
2 teaspoons coriander
1 teaspoon red pepper flakes
1/2 cup sesame seeds

Rinse the chicken and pat dry. Place in a bowl or sealable plastic bag. Purée the garlic, gingerroot, onion, soy sauce, lemon juice, sesame oil, sugar, salt, coriander and red pepper flakes in a blender or food processor. Pour over the chicken, coating the drumettes. Cover the bowl or seal the bag. Chill for 2 hours or longer; drain. Arrange in a single layer on a foil-lined 10×15-inch baking pan. Sprinkle with half of the sesame seeds. Broil, under a preheated broiler, for 5 to 6 minutes. Turn and sprinkle with the remaining sesame seeds. Broil for an additional 5 to 6 minutes or until cooked through, watching carefully to avoid burning. You may bake at 375 degrees for 15 minutes and then broil until crisp.

Yield: 36 drumettes

Bleu Cheese Puffs

1 (10-count) can refrigerated biscuits
6 tablespoons butter, softened
2 ounces bleu cheese

Cut each biscuit into quarters. Arrange in a 9-inch round pan. Heat the butter and bleu cheese in a saucepan until melted, stirring frequently. Pour over the biscuits. Bake at 400 degrees for 10 minutes or until brown.

Yield: 10 to 15 servings

Irish Soda Bread

4¹/2 cups flour
1   teaspoon salt
4   teaspoons baking powder
¹/2 teaspoon baking soda
3   tablespoons sugar
1   tablespoon caraway seeds
1   cup raisins
2   cups buttermilk
     Melted butter for brushing bread

Combine the flour, salt, baking powder, baking soda and sugar in a large bowl and mix well. Stir in the caraway seeds and raisins. Add the buttermilk and mix until a soft dough forms. Knead on a floured surface for 3 to 5 minutes or until smooth and elastic. Shape into a smooth round loaf. Press evenly into a greased and floured 9-inch round pan. Cut a ¹/2-inch-deep cross into the top.

Bake at 350 degrees for 1¹/4 hours or until bread sounds hollow when tapped on the bottom. Remove from the pan. Brush the top with butter. Place on a wire rack to cool completely.

Yield: 1 loaf

Evelyn's little dog was always included in the party festivities. For special occasions she even adorned him with a diamond bracelet as a collar.

99

Creamy Avocado Potage

1/2	cup sliced almonds, toasted	1/8	teaspoon seasoned salt
1 1/2	cups cold chicken broth	1/8	teaspoon white pepper
2	avocados, chopped		Whipped cream or sour
1/2	garlic clove		cream for garnish
1 1/2	cups cold chicken broth	1/4	cup sliced almonds, toasted
1/2	cup half-and-half		for garnish

Finely chop 1/2 cup almonds in a food processor. Add 1 1/2 cups chicken broth, avocados and garlic. Process until smooth. Add 1 1/2 cups chicken broth, half-and-half, salt and white pepper. Process until smooth. Ladle into soup bowls. Garnish with whipped cream or sour cream. Sprinkle 1/4 cup almonds over the top. You may serve this hot with a lemon wedge for garnish.

Yield: 2 to 4 servings

Somerset Roasted Carrot Soup

1 1/2	pounds unpeeled carrots
	Salt and pepper to taste
1/2	teaspoon unsalted butter
1	onion, chopped
1	teaspoon nutmeg
2	tablespoons honey
2	cups chicken stock
	Croutons or carrot curls for garnish

Cut the tops and bottoms off the carrots. Place in a roasting pan. Sprinkle with salt and pepper. Bake at 350 degrees for 30 minutes; do not allow to become too brown. Cut the carrots into large pieces.

Heat the butter in a soup pot until melted. Add the onion. Cook over low heat; do not brown. Add the nutmeg, honey and carrots. Cook for 2 minutes. Add the stock. Bring to a simmer. Simmer for 20 minutes. Purée in a blender. Season with salt and pepper. Ladle into 4 soup bowls. Garnish with croutons or carrot curls. May be served hot or cold.

Yield: 4 servings

Broccoli Leek Soup

1	bunch broccoli
3	tablespoons butter
1	cup coarsely chopped onion
1	cup chopped celery
2	leeks, chopped
2	russet potatoes, peeled, chopped
6	cups chicken stock
	Salt and pepper to taste
	Dash of hot pepper sauce
1	cup half-and-half
	Fresh parsley leaves for garnish

Rinse and trim the broccoli. Peel the stems and cut into slices. Cut the broccoli head into florets. Set aside some of the florets for garnish. Heat the butter in a large soup pot. Add the onion, celery and leeks. Cook until tender; do not brown. Add the broccoli, potatoes and stock. Bring to a boil. Season with salt and pepper. Add the hot red pepper sauce. Reduce the heat.

Simmer, covered, for 20 to 30 minutes or until broccoli is tender. Remove from the heat and let stand until cool.

Purée the soup in small batches in a blender until almost smooth. Chill until ready to serve. Stir in the half-and-half. Ladle into soup bowls. Garnish with reserved broccoli florets and parsley.

Yield: 6 to 8 servings

Mrs. Bartlett loved to tell about her pet macaw, Jingo, who, when Frederic was in his studio painting, would imitate her voice by calling, "Frederic, Frederic, telephone." Then the macaw would laugh.

During the 1930s, Evelyn Bartlett had pet monkeys who often accompanied her on her daily walks around the lagoon. However, it was squirrel monkeys who escaped from a neighboring club in the 1960s that established what is now a colony of monkeys who play among the trees at Bonnet House. Although native to Central and South America, they seem well adapted to their home in Fort Lauderdale.

Potato Soup au Vin

4   cups chopped peeled Idaho potatoes (about 2 or 3 large potatoes)
1   cup chopped onion
2   (14-ounce) cans chicken broth
1   cup water
1   cup white wine
1   teaspoon salt
    White pepper to taste
1   tablespoon butter or margarine
    Half-and-half or skim milk
    Bacon bits, chopped scallions, sour cream or
    shredded cheese for garnish

Combine the potatoes, onion, broth and water in a large saucepan. Cook over medium-high heat for 25 minutes. Add the wine, salt, white pepper and butter. Reduce the temperature to medium-low. Cook until potatoes are tender. Add enough half-and-half to make of the desired consistency. Ladle into soup bowls. Garnish with bacon bits, scallions, sour cream or shredded cheese.

Yield: 4 to 6 servings

Variations: **Cheese Soup**—Add 1 cup shredded cheese such as American or Cheddar. **Broccoli Soup**—Add one 10-ounce package thawed frozen broccoli florets and purée before serving

Red Bell Pepper Soup

3 tablespoons butter
4 red bell peppers, chopped
2 leeks, white part only, chopped
1 carrot, sliced
1 onion, chopped
2 cups chicken stock
2 cups heavy cream
  Salt and pepper to taste
  Finely chopped red bell pepper, parsley or chives for garnish

Heat the butter in a soup pot until melted. Add the bell peppers, leeks, carrot and onion. Sauté until tender. Pour in the stock and heavy cream. Reduce the heat. Simmer for 30 minutes. Purée in a blender. Return to the soup pot. Simmer for 15 minutes or longer. Season with salt and pepper. Ladle into soup bowls. Garnish with finely chopped red bell pepper, parsley or chives.

Yield: 4 to 6 servings

"Blue Ribbon" Split Pea Soup

1 ham bone with drippings and meat, from a honey-baked ham
1 large onion, chopped
1 large carrot, grated
1 (6-ounce) package split pea soup mix
1 (16-ounce) package green split peas
1 (12-ounce) package yellow split peas

Combine the ham bone, onion, carrot, pea soup mix and split peas in a soup pot. Add enough water to cover the bone. Bring to a simmer. Simmer, covered, for 4 hours or until bone falls apart and ham falls off the bone. Remove from the heat and cool slightly. Remove the bone and ham, discarding the bone. Let stand until cool. Cut the ham into bite-size pieces. Return the ham to the soup. Cook until heated through.

Yield: 20 servings

Supper

Creamy Zucchini Soup

2 tablespoons finely chopped green onions
1 garlic clove, minced
1 pound zucchini, thinly sliced
2 tablespoons butter
1³/4 cups chicken broth
¹/2 teaspoon curry powder
¹/2 teaspoon salt
¹/2 cup heavy cream or half-and-half

Simmer the green onions, garlic and zucchini in the butter in a tightly covered saucepan for 15 to 20 minutes, stirring occasionally. Spoon into a blender container. Add the broth, curry powder, salt and cream and process until mixed well. May be served hot or cold. You may freeze the soup before adding the cream and then add the cream to the thawed soup when ready to serve.

Yield: 4 servings

Chicken Cheese Corn Chowder

2 boneless skinless chicken breasts
1¹/2 cups white wine
1 white or red potato, peeled, chopped
¹/2 onion, chopped
1 (14-ounce) can cream-style corn
1 (15-ounce) can whole-kernel corn
1 (10-ounce) can cream of mushroom soup
1 (10-ounce) can cream of chicken soup
¹/4 cup chopped drained pimento
1 (8-ounce) package shredded Colby and Monterey Jack cheese blend

Combine the chicken, wine, potato and onion in a large saucepan. Bring to a boil. Reduce the heat. Simmer for 20 minutes or until chicken is cooked through. Remove the chicken and set aside. Add the corn, soups and pimento and mix well. Cook over low heat, stirring constantly. Cut the chicken into bite-size pieces. Stir into the chowder. Stir in half of the cheese. Ladle into 6 soup bowls. Garnish with the remaining cheese.

Yield: 6 servings

Supper

Couscous Salad

1	tablespoon butter
1	cup chicken stock
1	cup couscous
1	cup chopped celery, strings removed
1/2	cup pine nuts, toasted
1/2	cup raisins
1/4	cup chopped fresh flat-leaf parsley
1/4	teaspoon cinnamon
2	tablespoons sesame oil
4	scallions, thinly sliced
	Juice of 1 lemon
	Salt and pepper to taste

Heat the butter in a saucepan until melted. Add the stock and bring to a boil. Stir in the couscous. Remove from the heat. Let stand, covered, for 5 minutes.

Spoon the couscous into a nonreactive bowl and fluff to break up any lumps. Add the celery, pine nuts, raisins, parsley, cinnamon, sesame oil, scallions and lemon juice and toss to combine. Season with salt and pepper. Adjust seasonings to taste. May be served warm or chilled.

Yield: 6 servings

While sitting at her husband's bedside as he recovered from cataract surgery, Mrs. Bartlett sketched his folded hands. He recognized her attention to exactness and detail and encouraged her to paint, thus beginning her five-year painting period.

Orzo Salad with Sesame Dressing

Salt to taste
1 (16-ounce) package orzo
1 tablespoon sesame oil
4 carrots, julienned
2 cups raisins
1 cup sunflower seed kernels, toasted

Sesame Dressing
2 tablespoons chopped fresh parsley
2 tablespoons sliced green onions

Bring a large saucepan of water to a boil. Sprinkle in the salt. Add the orzo. Cook for 8 minutes; drain and rinse with cold water. Combine with the sesame oil in a bowl and toss gently to coat. Layer the orzo, carrots, raisins and sunflower seed kernels $1/2$ at a time in a large glass bowl. Drizzle 1 cup of the Sesame Dressing over the salad. Combine the parsley and green onions in a bowl and mix well. Sprinkle over the salad. Serve with the remaining dressing.

Yield: 10 servings

Sesame Dressing

$3/4$ cup corn oil
$1/2$ cup rice vinegar
$1/4$ cup sesame oil
1 tablespoon salt
1 tablespoon sugar
2 tablespoons grated orange zest

1 teaspoon pepper
1 teaspoon minced fresh gingerroot
1 teaspoon soy sauce
$1/2$ teaspoon minced garlic
$1/4$ teaspoon dried crushed red pepper

Process the corn oil, vinegar, sesame oil, salt, sugar, orange zest, pepper, gingerroot, soy sauce, garlic and red pepper in a blender or food processor until smooth.

Quinoa Salad

²/₃ cup quinoa
¹/₃ cup soy sauce
3 tablespoons lemon juice
2 tablespoons olive oil
1 tablespoon minced cilantro
¹/₃ cup minced mint leaves
¹/₃ cup minced chives
1 teaspoon ginger
1 teaspoon minced garlic
2 cups chopped tomatoes
2 cups chopped peeled jicama
  Greens

Cook the quinoa using the package directions; drain and rinse. Combine with the soy sauce, lemon juice, olive oil, cilantro, mint leaves, chives, ginger and garlic in a bowl and mix well. Add the tomatoes and jicama and toss to combine. Chill, covered, for 4 hours or longer. Serve on a bed of greens.

Yield: 8 servings

Evelyn painted from 1933 to 1938, then stopped to arrange the details of the debut of her daughter, Evie Lilly, and the managing of the large Bothways farm. During the '30s, her paintings were shown in galleries in Philadelphia, New York, Indianapolis, Toledo, and Washington, D.C. An exhibition of both Frederic and Evelyn's work was mounted at the Smithsonian Institution in 1982.

Warm Bean and Potato Salad

1   pound small red potatoes, cut into $^{1}/_{4}$-inch slices
8   ounces fresh green beans, cut into 1-inch pieces
    Mustard Dressing
1   small onion, coarsely chopped
2   bacon slices, chopped

Combine the potatoes with enough water to cover in a saucepan. Bring to a boil. Boil for 5 minutes. Add the beans. Boil for 3 to 5 minutes or until potatoes are just tender. Drain and place in a serving bowl. Add the Mustard Dressing and toss gently to coat.

Sauté the onion and bacon in a small skillet until bacon is crisp. Remove and place on paper towels to drain. Sprinkle over the top of the salad.

Yield: 6 servings

Mustard Dressing

1   teaspoon Dijon mustard
1   teaspoon sugar
2   tablespoons red wine vinegar
2   tablespoons virgin olive oil
$^{1}/_{2}$ teaspoon dillweed
     Salt and pepper to taste

Whisk the mustard, sugar, vinegar, olive oil, dillweed, salt and pepper together in a bowl.

Bow Tie Bistro Salad

1   (16-ounce) package bow tie pasta, cooked, drained
1¹/₂ pounds boneless skinless chicken breasts, cooked, chopped
1   large red onion, thinly sliced
1   large tomato, chopped
1   (4-ounce) can sliced black olives, drained
8   ounces feta cheese, crumbled
1   (10-ounce) package fresh spinach, rinsed
1   cup marinated artichoke hearts, sliced
    Tomato Vinaigrette

Combine the pasta, chicken, onion, tomato, olives, cheese, spinach and artichoke hearts in a large bowl and mix well. Pour the Tomato Vinaigrette over the salad and toss to combine.

Yield: 8 servings

Tomato Vinaigrette

2   ounces sun-dried tomatoes
1   garlic clove
1   tablespoon tomato paste
³/₄ cup olive oil
6   tablespoons balsamic vinegar
    Salt and pepper to taste

Process the sun-dried tomatoes, garlic, tomato paste, olive oil, vinegar, salt and pepper in a blender until smooth.

After buying a large basket of fruit on one of the Caribbean islands, Frederic describes the longevity of the produce: "Mrs. Bartlett painted ten watercolors. Then I was free to eat the fruit. As still further proof of our economy, we saved the seeds and have planted them at our Florida place."

Chicken Salad with Dates

3	cups chopped cooked chicken
1	cup chopped dates
1	cup chopped celery
1/4	cup Italian dressing
1/3	cup mayonnaise
1	teaspoon curry powder
1	teaspoon Worcestershire sauce
1/2	teaspoon salt
1/8	teaspoon pepper
	Lettuce
1/2	cup salted cashew nuts

Combine the chicken, dates and celery in a bowl and mix well. Combine the dressing, mayonnaise, curry powder, Worcestershire sauce, salt and pepper in a bowl and mix well. Pour over the chicken mixture and toss to coat.

Chill, covered, for 8 to 12 hours. Arrange the lettuce on a serving plate. Spoon the salad over the lettuce. Sprinkle the cashew nuts over the top.

Yield: 6 to 8 servings

Chicken Salad with Herb Dressing

2   cups seedless grapes
2   cups chopped cooked chicken breast
1   cup thinly sliced red bell pepper
1   cup thinly sliced yellow bell pepper
1/2 cup sliced snow peas
1/2 cup sliced jicama
3   tablespoons slivered almonds, toasted
2   tablespoons chopped green onions
4   cups cooked pasta such as bow tie, spiral or shell
    Herb Dressing

Combine the grapes, chicken, bell peppers, snow peas, jicama, almonds, green onions, pasta and Herb Dressing in a large bowl and toss to combine.

Yield: 4 to 6 servings

Herb Dressing

1/2 cup low-fat mayonnaise
1/2 cup plain low-fat yogurt
2   teaspoons salt
1   teaspoon Dijon mustard
2   tablespoons sugar
1   teaspoon tarragon
1   teaspoon thyme
1/4 teaspoon pepper
1/4 teaspoon rosemary

Whisk the mayonnaise, yogurt, salt, mustard, sugar, tarragon, thyme, pepper and rosemary together in a bowl.

Chicken and Wild Rice Salad

1   cup pecan pieces
     Butter
1   (6-ounce) package Uncle Ben's long grain and wild rice mix
1   cup chicken broth
3   cups chopped cooked chicken
1   red bell pepper, julienned
3/4 cup chopped arugula
1/2 cup chopped green onions
     Soy Dressing
     Large escarole leaves for garnish

Sauté the pecans in a small amount of butter. Prepare the rice using the package directions and substituting the chicken broth for 1 cup of the water. Combine the rice, pecans, chicken, bell pepper, arugula and green onions in a bowl and mix well. Pour the Soy Dressing over the salad and toss to combine. Garnish with escarole leaves.

Yield: 6 to 8 servings

Soy Dressing

4 1/2   teaspoons soy sauce
2   tablespoons rice wine vinegar
4 1/2   teaspoons sesame oil
1/4   teaspoon salt
1/4   teaspoon pepper

Place the soy sauce, vinegar, sesame oil, salt and pepper in a covered jar and shake to combine.

Chicken Pasta Charmer

6	chicken breasts (about 1½ pounds)		1	(15-ounce) can garbanzo beans, drained
1	onion, cut into quarters		8	ounces fresh mushrooms, sliced
1	carrot, cut into halves		1	(4-ounce) can pitted black olives, drained
4	celery ribs, cut into halves		1	(6-ounce) jar marinated artichoke hearts, drained
⅓	cup pine nuts			Red Wine Vinegar Dressing
1	tablespoon butter			
⅓	pound snow peas			
16	ounces shell pasta			
1	red bell pepper, julienned			

Combine the chicken, onion, carrot and celery with enough water to cover in a saucepan. Bring to a boil. Boil until chicken is cooked through. Drain, discarding the onion, carrot and celery. Cut the chicken into bite-size pieces. Sauté the pine nuts in the butter in a small skillet until brown. Let stand until cool. Bring enough water to cover the snow peas to a boil in a saucepan. Add the snow peas. Cook for 1 minute; drain. Let stand until cool. Cook the pasta until al dente using the package directions. Drain and rinse in cold water.

Combine the chicken, pine nuts, snow peas, pasta, bell pepper, beans, mushrooms, olives and artichoke hearts in a large bowl and toss to combine. Pour Red Wine Vinegar Dressing over the salad and toss to coat. Chill, covered, until ready to serve. You may prepare this dish up to 1 day in advance.

Yield: 12 servings

Red Wine Vinegar Dressing

1	cup olive oil		1½	teaspoons salt
5	tablespoons red wine vinegar		1	teaspoon pepper
½	cup chopped parsley		½	teaspoon curry powder
4	teaspoons Dijon mustard		½	teaspoon garlic powder

Place the olive oil, vinegar, parsley, mustard, salt, pepper, curry powder and garlic powder in a covered jar and shake until combined.

The Weinhardt Gallery at Bonnet House, once a suite of guest rooms, was created to showcase the art of Evelyn Bartlett. Though not a formally trained artist, Mrs. Bartlett produced a body of work of exceptional charm that is invaluable as a record of the lives of the Bartletts. Her husband said of her, ". . . painting has been going on with eye and mind most of her life. My most successful artistic venture was the discovery of the art of Evelyn Bartlett."

Grilled Chicken and Pear Salad

4   boneless skinless chicken breasts
     Orange Honey Dressing
2   Anjou pears, cut into 8 wedges
1   cup pecan pieces
8   cups mixed salad greens

Combine the chicken and $^1/_4$ cup Orange Honey Dressing in a sealable plastic bag. Combine the pears and $^1/_4$ cup Orange Honey Dressing in a sealable plastic bag. Chill the chicken and pears for 10 minutes to 8 hours. Place the pecans on a baking sheet. Bake at 325 degrees for 15 minutes, stirring once.

Drain the chicken reserving the marinade. Place on a grill over hot coals. Grill until juices run clear, basting with the reserved marinade.

Drain the pears reserving the marinade. Grill the pears for 4 to 5 minutes, basting with the reserved marinade.

Toss the greens with the remaining Orange Honey Dressing in a bowl. Divide among 4 plates. Slice the chicken breasts thinly. Arrange the chicken, pears and pecans over the greens. Serve immediately.

Yield: 4 servings

Orange Honey Dressing

$^1/_2$ cup walnut or olive oil
$^1/_4$ cup balsamic vinegar
$^1/_4$ cup fresh orange juice
$^1/_4$ cup chopped cilantro
2   tablespoons honey
$^1/_2$ teaspoon Asian or Caribbean chili sauce
1   garlic clove, minced
$^1/_2$ teaspoon salt

Whisk the walnut oil, vinegar, orange juice, cilantro, honey, chili sauce, garlic and salt together in a bowl.

Supper

Paella Salad

1   (7-ounce) package yellow rice mix
1/3 cup vegetable oil
2   tablespoons tarragon vinegar
1/8 teaspoon salt
8   cups water
1/8 teaspoon mustard
1   teaspoon Old Bay seasoning
1   cup unpeeled fresh shrimp
2   cups chopped cooked chicken
1   tomato, peeled, seeded, chopped
1   green bell pepper, chopped
1/2 cup minced onion
1/3 cup chopped celery
1   tablespoon salt
1   pound cooked chopped smoked sausage (optional)
1/2 cup black olives (optional)
1   cup frozen baby English peas, thawed

Cook the rice using the package directions. Combine the oil, vinegar and salt in a small bowl and mix well. Stir into the cooked rice. Let stand until room temperature.

Bring the water to a boil in a saucepan. Add the mustard, Old Bay seasoning and shrimp. Cook until shrimp turn pink. Drain, peel and devein the shrimp.

Combine the rice mixture, shrimp, chicken, tomato, bell pepper, onion, celery, salt, sausage, olives and peas in a large bowl and toss to combine. Chill, covered, in the refrigerator.

Yield: 8 servings

While a young art student in Germany, Frederic wrote in his journal: "And so much of our Munich life was filled with close friendships, with art in so many of its forms outside of my chosen one, glorious music, interesting plays and all the cosmopolitan life that goes on in Munich which, although small, is never provincial."

Supper

Tropical Salad with Peach Schnapps Dressing

Boston or green leaf lettuce
1 pound cooked turkey, chicken or ham, julienned
1 large red bell pepper, chopped
2 papayas, peeled, sliced or 1 large cantaloupe, sliced
1^1/$_2$ cups seedless red grapes (about 1 large bunch)
^{1}/$_4$ cup chopped fresh parsley
    Peach Schnapps Dressing

Line a serving plate with the lettuce leaves. Combine the turkey, bell pepper, papayas, grapes and parsley in a bowl and mix well. Add the Peach Schnapps Dressing and toss to combine. Spoon over the lettuce leaves.

Yield: *4 to 6 servings*

Peach Schnapps Dressing

1 cup mayonnaise
1 teaspoon Dijon mustard
^{1}/$_2$ cup peach schnapps
    Pinch of salt

Whisk the mayonnaise and mustard together in a small bowl. Whisk in the schnapps and salt gradually. Chill, covered, until ready to serve.

Chili Salsa Beef

1 1/2 pounds boneless chuck
1 tablespoon vegetable oil
1 cup chunky salsa
2 tablespoons brown sugar
1 tablespoon soy sauce
1 garlic clove, crushed
1/3 cup chopped cilantro
2 tablespoons lime juice

Cut the beef into 1-inch pieces. Brown on all sides in hot oil in a large skillet; drain. Stir in the salsa, brown sugar, soy sauce and garlic. Bring to a boil. Reduce the heat. Simmer, covered, for 1 hour. Remove the cover.

Cook over low heat for an additional 30 minutes or until tender. Remove from the heat. Stir in the cilantro and lime juice. Serve over hot cooked rice.

Yield: 6 to 8 servings

Frederic was commissioned to do a frieze depicting medieval athletic games in the Frank Dickinson Bartlett Memorial Gymnasium, named in honor of his brother, at the University of Chicago.

117

Ham Loaf

1   *pound ground ham*
2   *pounds ground pork*
1¹/2 *cups rolled oats or bread crumbs*
1   *onion, chopped*
¹/2 *cup chopped fresh parsley*
2   *eggs*
1   *cup milk*
     Salt and pepper to taste
     Basting Sauce

Combine the ham, pork, oats, onion, parsley, eggs, milk, salt and pepper in a bowl and mix well. Shape into a loaf and place on a baking pan or press into a loaf pan. Bake in a preheated 400-degree oven for 15 to 20 minutes. Drain the drippings. Reduce the oven temperature to 325 degrees. Bake for an additional 45 minutes, basting with Basting Sauce every 15 minutes. Serve with a mustard sauce.

Yield: 10 to 12 servings

Basting Sauce

1   *teaspoon grated fresh gingerroot*
1   *teaspoon butter*
1   *cup packed brown sugar*
1   *tablespoon prepared mustard*
¹/4 *cup cider vinegar*
¹/4 *cup water or orange juice*

Sauté the gingerroot in the butter in a skillet. Stir in the brown sugar, mustard, vinegar and water.

Frederic wrote in his journal: "To think that men could conceive such things, and actually bring them into being on a flat bare canvas; could create illusions of space, perspective, sunlight or storm, all on a piece of cloth with colors taken from dark mines or pungent earth, applied by means of bristles taken from a pig's back fastened to a little stick."

Luscious Lamb Shanks

4   lamb shanks
4   or 5 garlic cloves
1   tablespoon salt
1   tablespoon pepper
1/4 cup water
2   or 3 white onions, sliced
1/2 envelope onion soup mix

Rinse the lamb shanks and pat dry. Cut small pockets in the meatiest portion of each shank and insert the garlic cloves. Combine the salt and pepper in a small bowl and mix well. Sprinkle over the lamb. Arrange the lamb in a shallow baking pan. Pour the water into the pan. Arrange the onion slices over the lamb. Sprinkle the soup mix over the top. Bake, covered, at 350 degrees for 2 1/4 hours or until lamb is tender.

Yield: 4 servings

Pecan Chicken

1/4 cup honey
1/4 cup Dijon mustard
4   boneless skinless chicken breast halves
1   cup chopped pecans

Combine the honey and mustard in a bowl and mix well. Brush over both sides of the chicken. Dip the chicken in the pecans to coat. Place in a shallow greased baking dish. Bake at 350 degrees for 30 to 40 minutes or until cooked through.

Yield: 4 servings

Turkey Meat Loaf with Sun-Dried Tomatoes

1   pound ground turkey
1   onion, chopped
1   cup fresh bread crumbs
1   egg, beaten
1/2 cup pine nuts, toasted
12   oil-packed sun-dried tomatoes, drained, chopped
1/3 cup milk
2   teaspoons chopped fresh rosemary, or
     1/2 teaspoon dried crumbled rosemary
2   teaspoons chopped fresh oregano, or
     1/2 teaspoon dried crumbled oregano
     Salt and pepper to taste

Combine the turkey, onion, bread crumbs, egg, pine nuts, tomatoes, milk, rosemary and oregano in a bowl and mix well. Season with salt and pepper. Press into a 5×9-inch loaf pan. Bake at 375 degrees for 50 minutes or until loaf pulls away from sides of pan and is golden brown.

Yield: 4 to 6 servings

Baked Snapper Fillets

2   large onions, finely chopped
1/4   cup olive oil
2   garlic cloves, sliced
1   cup chopped celery
1   cup chopped carrots
1/2   cup chopped parsley
1   (28-ounce) can tomatoes
1/2   teaspoon salt
1/2   teaspoon pepper
6   snapper fillets
       Juice of 1 lemon

Sauté the onions in hot olive oil in a skillet. Add the garlic, celery, carrots and parsley and mix well. Add the tomatoes. Bring to a simmer. Simmer for 5 minutes. Season with salt and pepper. Arrange the snapper in a baking dish. Spoon the sauce over the snapper. Drizzle the lemon juice evenly over the top. Bake at 350 degrees for 10 minutes per inch of thickness of the snapper or until fish flakes easily.

Yield: 6 servings

Shrimp Madrid

1   cup (2 sticks) butter
1   (12-ounce) bottle chili sauce
1   teaspoon Worcestershire sauce
3   tablespoons sherry
       Salt and pepper to taste
1 1/2 pounds shrimp, cooked, peeled

Place the butter, chili sauce and Worcestershire sauce in the top of a double boiler over simmering water. Cook until butter is melted, stirring frequently. Stir in the sherry. Season with salt and pepper. Stir in the shrimp. Cook for 30 minutes or until heated through; do not boil. Serve over hot cooked rice.

Yield: 4 servings

Supper

Sparkling Scampi

3	tablespoons vegetable oil
3	tablespoons butter
6	large garlic cloves, chopped
2	shallots, chopped
3	large tomatoes, finely chopped
	Salt and black pepper to taste
	Pinch of crushed red pepper flakes (optional)
1	pound large shrimp, peeled
4	ounces fresh bay scallops
	Juice of 1 lemon
	Dash of Champagne or dry white wine

Combine the oil, butter, garlic and shallots in a large skillet. Sauté over low heat until garlic and shallots are tender. Stir in the tomatoes and sauté for 20 minutes.

Stir the salt, black pepper and red pepper into the skillet. Bring to a boil. Add the shrimp and scallops. Cook for 6 minutes or until shrimp turn pink, stirring occasionally. Stir in the lemon juice and Champagne.

Yield: 4 servings

Supper

Antipasti Peppers

Roasted red bell peppers, peeled, sliced
Salt
Extra-virgin olive oil
Balsamic vinegar (optional)

Combine the desired amount of bell peppers, salt, olive oil and vinegar and toss to combine. Serve at room temperature.

Yield: Variable

Roasted Red Bell Peppers

Red bell peppers

Method I: Hold the bell pepper with tongs directly over a gas flame until the bell pepper blisters, turning often. Place the bell pepper in a plastic bag; seal. Let stand until cool. Remove the skin from the bell pepper. Repeat with any remaining bell peppers.

Large red bell peppers

Method II: Cut each bell pepper in half lengthwise. Remove the seeds and stem. Place, cut-side down, on a foil-lined baking sheet. Broil until the skin blisters. Place the bell peppers in a plastic bag; seal. Let stand until cool. Remove the skin from the bell peppers.

Large red bell peppers

Method III: Cut each bell pepper in half lengthwise. Remove the seeds and stem. Place, cut-side down, on a foil-lined baking sheet. Bake at 400 degrees until the skin blisters. Place the bell peppers in a plastic bag; seal. Let stand until cool. Remove the skin from the bell peppers.

Supper

Fresh Tomato Tart

1   unbaked (10- to 12-inch) pie shell
1/3 cup Dijon mustard
2   cups shredded mozzarella or firm goat cheese, such as Holland
2   large tomatoes, cut into wedges
     Dash of garlic powder
1   tablespoon oregano
     Salt and pepper to taste
1   tablespoon olive oil

Brush the pie shell with mustard. Arrange the cheese evenly over the bottom of the shell. Arrange the tomato wedges in a decorative fashion over the cheese. Sprinkle the garlic powder, oregano, salt and pepper over the tomatoes. Drizzle the olive oil over the top. Bake at 400 degrees for 45 minutes. You may substitute 1 zucchini cut into slices for 1 of the tomatoes.

Yield: 8 to 10 servings

Vidalia Onion Pie

1/2 cup (1 stick) butter
2   pounds Vidalia onions, thinly sliced
3   eggs, beaten
1   cup sour cream
1/2 teaspoon pepper
1/4 teaspoon salt
1/4 teaspoon hot sauce
1   unbaked (9-inch) pie shell
1/2 cup grated Parmesan cheese

Heat the butter in a skillet until melted. Add the onions. Cook until tender; do not brown. Combine the eggs and sour cream in a bowl and mix well. Stir into the onions. Add the pepper, salt and hot sauce and mix well. Spoon into the pie shell. Bake in a preheated 450-degree oven for 20 minutes. Sprinkle the Parmesan cheese over the top. Reduce the heat to 325 degrees. Bake for an additional 20 minutes.

Yield: 6 servings

Supper

Basil Roasted Vegetables over Couscous

2	tablespoons minced fresh basil
2	tablespoons balsamic vinegar
1	tablespoon extra-virgin olive oil
$1/4$	teaspoon salt
2	garlic cloves, crushed
2	zucchini, cut into 1-inch pieces
1	red bell pepper, cut into 1-inch pieces
1	yellow bell pepper, cut into 1-inch pieces
1	red onion, cut into 8 wedges
8	ounces mushrooms
3	cups hot cooked couscous
1	(3-ounce) package basil-flavored chèvre, crumbled (optional)
$1/8$	teaspoon pepper
	Fresh basil sprigs for garnish

Combine the basil, vinegar, olive oil, salt and garlic in a large bowl and mix well. Add the zucchini, bell peppers, onion and mushrooms and toss to coat. Arrange in a single layer in a shallow roasting pan.

Bake at 425 degrees for 35 minutes or until tender and brown, stirring occasionally. Place the couscous in a serving bowl. Spoon the vegetables over the couscous. Sprinkle the chèvre over the vegetables. Sprinkle with pepper. Garnish with fresh basil sprigs.

Yield: 4 servings

Frederic had two sisters, each of whom established a museum in the Southwest. Florence Bartlett founded the Museum of International Folk Art in Santa Fe, New Mexico, and gave it to the state. Maie Bartlett Heard and her husband Dwight founded the Heard Museum in Phoenix, Arizona.

Chile Rice Casserole

3   cups cooked rice
    Salt and freshly ground pepper to taste
3   cups sour cream
1   teaspoon salt
2   (4-ounce) cans chopped green chiles
12 ounces Monterey Jack cheese, cut into strips
1/2 cup shredded Cheddar cheese

Season the rice with salt and pepper to taste. Combine the sour cream, 1 teaspoon salt and green chiles in a bowl and mix well. Spread one third of the rice over the bottom of a buttered 1 1/2-quart baking dish. Layer the sour cream mixture, Monterey Jack cheese and remaining rice 1/2 at a time in the prepared dish. Bake at 350 degrees for 40 minutes or until heated through. Sprinkle the Cheddar cheese over the top. Return to the oven. Cook until the Cheddar cheese is melted.

Yield: 6 servings

Mexican Macaroni

1   (8-ounce) package macaroni
1   (14-ounce) can Mexican-style tomatoes, chopped
1   (10-ounce) can cream of mushroom soup
1   cup sour cream
1   (4-ounce) can chopped green chiles
1   cup shredded Monterey Jack cheese
1   cup shredded sharp Cheddar cheese

Cook the macaroni using the package directions; drain. Combine the cooked macaroni, tomatoes, soup, sour cream and green chiles in a bowl and mix well. Stir in 1/2 cup of the Monterey Jack cheese and 1/2 cup of the Cheddar cheese. Spoon into a greased 2-quart baking dish. Sprinkle the remaining Monterey Jack cheese and Cheddar cheese over the top. Bake at 350 degrees for 30 minutes.

Yield: 8 servings

Supper

Bread Pudding with Amaretto Sauce

1   pound sweet, egg or yellow bread such as Hawaiian
4   cups half-and-half
3   eggs
1   cup sugar
2   tablespoons vanilla extract
1   teaspoon almond extract
     Amaretto Sauce

Cut the bread into 2-inch cubes. Arrange evenly on a baking sheet. Broil until lightly toasted. Let stand for 1 hour or longer.

Place the bread and half-and-half in a large bowl and toss to combine. Let stand until bread is moistened and half-and-half is absorbed. Whisk the eggs, sugar, vanilla and almond extract together in a bowl. Stir into the bread mixture. Spoon into a buttered 9×13-inch baking dish. Bake at 325 degrees for 1 hour or until a knife inserted in the center comes out clean and top is golden brown. Let stand until room temperature. Cut into squares and place on individual dessert plates. Spoon Amaretto Sauce over the top.

Yield: 12 servings

Amaretto Sauce

1   cup (2 sticks) butter
2   cups confectioners' sugar
6   tablespoons amaretto
4   egg yolks

Heat the butter in the top of a double boiler over simmering water until melted. Whisk in the sugar gradually. Cook until mixture is creamy, whisking constantly. Whisk in the amaretto. Whisk in the eggs 1 at a time. Cook until sauce is the consistency of honey and measures 160 degrees on a thermometer, stirring constantly.

Sunday Afternoon on the Island of Grande Jatte by Georges Seurat was among a number of important paintings given to the Chicago Art Institute by Frederic in 1926 in memory of his wife Helen. They had purchased the Seurat in France in 1924 for $20,000. It hangs in the Bartlett Memorial Collection, where it is one of the Institute's most popular paintings.

Supper

Date Pudding

3/4 cup packed light brown sugar	1/2 teaspoon salt
3 eggs, beaten	1 1/2 cups chopped dates
3/4 cup packed light brown sugar	1 cup chopped walnuts
1/2 cup flour	1 teaspoon vanilla extract
2 teaspoons baking powder	

Stir 3/4 cup brown sugar gradually into the eggs in a bowl. Sift 3/4 cup brown sugar, flour, baking powder and salt together. Fold into the egg mixture. Stir in the dates, walnuts and vanilla. Spoon into a greased 7×10-inch baking pan. Bake at 350 degrees for 40 to 45 minutes; pudding will fall when removed from oven. Cut into squares and serve warm with whipped cream.

Yield: 12 servings

Spiked Apple Crisp

5 cups peeled sliced Pippin, Jonathan or Winesap apples	1/4 cup packed light brown sugar
1/2 teaspoon cinnamon-sugar	1/2 cup rolled oats
1 teaspoon grated lemon zest	1/4 cup sifted flour
1 teaspoon grated orange zest	1/4 teaspoon salt
1 ounce Grand Marnier	1/2 cup (1 stick) butter or margarine, melted
1 ounce amaretto	1/2 cup chopped pecans
3/4 cup sugar	

Arrange the apple slices in a greased 2-quart baking dish. Sprinkle with the cinnamon-sugar, lemon zest, orange zest, Grand Marnier and amaretto. Combine the sugar, brown sugar, oats, flour, salt, butter and pecans in a bowl and mix until crumbly. Sprinkle over the apples. Bake at 350 degrees for 1 hour. Serve with whipped cream or ice cream.

Yield: 6 to 8 servings

Creamy Coconut Pie

1	unbaked (9-inch) pie shell	$1/4$	teaspoon almond extract
$3/4$	cup sugar	1	cup whipping cream, chilled
3	tablespoons cornstarch	2	tablespoons confectioners'
	Dash of salt		sugar
2	cups milk	2	(4-ounce) cans flaked
3	egg yolks, beaten		coconut, or 2 cups grated
$3/4$	teaspoon vanilla extract		fresh coconut

Prick the pie shell several times. Bake at 450 degrees for 10 to 12 minutes. Cool on a wire rack.

Combine the sugar, cornstarch and salt in a heavy saucepan. Stir in the milk gradually. Bring to a boil over medium heat, stirring occasionally. Boil for 1 minute or until thickened, stirring constantly. Remove from the heat. Stir a small amount of the hot mixture into the beaten egg yolks. Stir the egg yolks into the hot mixture.

Cook for 3 minutes over low heat, stirring occasionally. Remove from the heat. Stir in the vanilla and almond extract. Pour into a small bowl. Cover the surface with waxed paper. Refrigerate for 1 hour or until chilled through.

Whip the cream and confectioners' sugar in a bowl until stiff peaks form. Chill, covered, until ready to use.

Pour the chilled filling into the pie crust. Sprinkle half of the coconut over the filling. Spread the sweetened whipped cream over the coconut. Sprinkle the remaining coconut over the whipped cream. Serve at once or chill for 1 hour or less.

Yield: 6 to 8 servings

Raspberry Ribbon Pie

1	(3-ounce) package raspberry gelatin
1/4	cup sugar
1 1/4	cups boiling water
1	(10-ounce) package frozen raspberries
1	tablespoon lemon juice
3	ounces cream cheese, softened
1/2	cup sifted confectioners' sugar
1	teaspoon vanilla extract
1/8	teaspoon salt
1	cup whipping cream, whipped
1	baked (9-inch) pie shell
	Whipped cream for garnish (optional)

Dissolve the gelatin and sugar in boiling water in a bowl. Add the raspberries and lemon juice. Stir until the berries thaw. Chill until partially set. Combine the cream cheese, confectioners' sugar, vanilla and salt in a bowl and mix until smooth. Fold in the whipped cream gradually. Layer the cream cheese mixture and raspberry mixture 1/2 at a time in the pie shell. Chill, covered, until set. Garnish with additional whipped cream.

Yield: 6 to 8 servings

Velvet Hammer

1	quart vanilla ice cream
1/2	cup brandy
1/3	cup Cointreau or Triple Sec
	Freshly grated nutmeg (optional)

Soften the ice cream in a microwave for 25 seconds. Combine the ice cream, brandy and Cointreau in a blender or food processor container. Process until smooth. Scoop into goblets or sherbet dishes. Sprinkle with nutmeg. May be prepared in advance and frozen. Let stand for 30 to 45 minutes. Stir before serving.

Yield: 4 to 6 servings

Coconut Dreams

1   cup (2 sticks) butter, softened
1/2   cup sugar
2   cups flour
1   (4-ounce) can flaked coconut

Cream the butter and sugar in a mixing bowl until light and fluffy. Beat in the flour and coconut. Shape into 2 logs 1 1/2-inches in diameter. Chill, covered, until firm. Cut the logs into 1/4-inch-thick slices. Place the slices on a nonstick cookie sheet. Bake at 300 degrees for 25 minutes or until coconut is browned. Cool on a wire rack. Store in an airtight container.

Yield: 5 dozen

Decadent Chocolate Cookies

6   tablespoons unsalted butter
8   ounces semisweet chocolate
3   ounces unsweetened chocolate
1/3   cup flour
1/4   teaspoon baking powder
1/4   teaspoon salt
3   eggs
1   cup sugar
2   teaspoons vanilla extract
2   cups semisweet chocolate chips
1   cup coarsely chopped pecans or walnuts

Heat the butter, semisweet and unsweetened chocolate in a heavy saucepan over medium-high heat until melted and smooth, stirring frequently. Let stand until cool. Sift the flour, baking powder and salt together. Beat the eggs, sugar and vanilla in a mixing bowl until light and fluffy. Stir in the chocolate mixture. Add the flour mixture and mix well. Stir in the chocolate chips and pecans. Drop by teaspoonfuls or tablespoonfuls onto a parchment-lined cookie sheet. Bake at 350 degrees for 10 to 12 minutes. Cool on a wire rack.

Yield: 4 to 7 dozen

Supper

Pageant Cookies

2	cups unbleached flour
1	teaspoon baking soda
1	teaspoon cinnamon
1	teaspoon ground ginger
¹/₂	teaspoon salt
1	cup (2 sticks) butter
1¹/₂	cups packed light brown sugar
1	egg, room temperature
1	teaspoon vanilla extract
2	cups semisweet chocolate chips
1	cup chopped nuts
1	cup confectioners' sugar

Combine the flour, baking soda, cinnamon, ginger and salt in a bowl and mix well. Cream the butter in a mixing bowl until light and fluffy. Beat the brown sugar, egg and vanilla into the butter. Add the flour mixture and mix well. Fold in the chocolate chips and nuts. Chill, covered, for up to 24 hours or until firm.

Shape into 1-inch balls. Dredge in confectioners' sugar. Place 2 inches apart on a greased or parchment-lined cookie sheet. Bake at 350 degrees for 8 minutes. Cool on the cookie sheet for 5 minutes. Remove to a wire rack to cool completely. Store in an airtight container.

Yield: 6 dozen

Caramel Brownies

1   (14-ounce) package caramels, unwrapped
²/₃ cup evaporated milk
1   (18-ounce) package German chocolate cake mix
³/₄ cup (1¹/₂ sticks) butter, softened
1   cup chopped nuts
1   cup semisweet chocolate chips

Combine the caramels and ¹/₃ cup of the evaporated milk in the top of a double boiler. Cook over simmering water until caramels have melted, stirring constantly. Remove from the heat.

Combine the remaining ¹/₃ cup evaporated milk, cake mix and butter in a mixing bowl. Beat until batter holds together. Stir in the nuts.

Press half of the cake mixture over the bottom of a greased 9×13-inch baking pan. Bake at 350 degrees for 6 minutes. Sprinkle chocolate chips over the baked layer. Spread the caramel mixture over the chocolate chips. Crumble the remaining cake mixture over the top. Bake for an additional 17 to 20 minutes. Cool in the pan. Chill for 30 minutes. Cut into squares.

Yield: 2¹/₂ dozen

"He was one of the kindest people I've ever known . . . a great companion, great fun, handsome . . . everything perfectly delightful about him."

—Evelyn Bartlett
describing Frederic

Kahlúa Nut Bars

¹/₂ cup (1 stick) butter, softened	1¹/₂ cups flour
2 eggs	2 tablespoons baking powder
2¹/₂ cups packed light brown sugar	1 teaspoon salt
¹/₄ cup Kahlúa	1 cup chopped nuts
1 teaspoon vanilla extract	1 (4-ounce) can flaked coconut

Combine the butter, eggs and brown sugar in a bowl and mix well. Add the Kahlúa, vanilla, flour, baking powder and salt and mix well. Stir in the nuts and coconut. Spoon into a greased 9×13-inch baking pan. Bake at 350 degrees for 25 minutes. Cool in the pan. Cut into squares.

Yield: 2 dozen

Sherried Walnuts

1¹/₂ cups sugar	3 cups walnuts
¹/₂ cup sweet sherry	¹/₂ teaspoon cinnamon

Combine the sugar and sherry in a saucepan and mix well. Cook over medium heat to 234 to 240 degrees on a candy thermometer, soft-ball stage. Remove from the heat. Add the walnuts and cinnamon. Stir until mixture becomes cloudy and sticks together. Spread onto a buttered baking sheet and separate walnuts quickly using 2 forks. Let stand until cool. Store in an airtight container.

Yield: 3 cups

Mincemeat Foldovers

2 cups flour
1/4 cup sugar
1/8 teaspoon salt
8 ounces cream cheese, softened
1 cup (2 sticks) butter, softened
1 cup prepared mincemeat
1 tablespoon rum
2 teaspoons light corn syrup
1 cup confectioners' sugar

Sift the flour, sugar and salt together in a bowl. Cut in the cream cheese and butter, working the dough until it forms a ball. Divide into 4 equal portions. Wrap each portion in plastic wrap. Chill for 2 to 12 hours.

Roll one of the dough portions into a 10-inch circle on a lightly floured surface. Cut with a 3-inch round cutter. Place 1 teaspoon of mincemeat in the center of each 3-inch circle. Fold each circle in half and pinch the edges together or crimp with a fork. Repeat with the remaining dough and mincemeat. Foldovers may be frozen at this point. Place foldovers on a baking sheet.

Bake at 350 degrees for 20 to 25 minutes. Stir the rum and corn syrup gradually into the confectioners' sugar in a bowl. Brush on the warm foldovers.

Yield: 4 dozen

Acknowledgements

Acknowledgements

Irene Hart
Barbara Keith
Marie Little
Carol Mulhall
Ellen Murton
Bill Sydnor
Mary & Jack Wilcox

The Bonnet House Staff

Robert Kauth, *Executive Director*
Susan Parker, *Business Manager*
Lisa Bova, *Director of Education*
Linda Calahan, *Director of Grant Programs*
Joanne Carey, *Special Events Coordinator*
Denyse Cunningham, *Curator*
Rose Francois, *Custodian*
Stacy Hyers, *Assistant Director of Education*
William Lugo, *General Maintenance Supervisor*
Larry Many, *Grounds Supervisor*
Linda Schaller, *Volunteer & Tour Coordinator*

Reference Publications

Available from Bonnet House

Reflections of a Legacy: The Bonnet House Story, by Jayne Rice

Bonnet House: The Life and Gift, by Jayne Thomas Rice

Bonnet House: Coastal Wilderness Refined, by Jayne Rice Workman

*African Americans Remember: Life in the 30s and Early 40s on the
Birch-Bartlett Properties*, by Lisa Bova and Kitty Oliver

Index

Index

Index

Index

Order Form
Entirely Entertaining
IN THE Bonnet House *Style*

Bonnet House Alliance
P.O. Box 460117
Fort Lauderdale, Florida 33346

Please send _____ copies of *Entirely Entertaining in the Bonnet House Style* at $22.95 per book $ _____

Sales tax (Florida residents only) at $1.38 per book $ _____

Shipping and handling at $4.00 per book $ _____

Total $ _____

_____
Name

_____
Street Address

_____
City   State   Zip

_____
Telephone Number

Method of Payment:
   [   ] AMEX   [   ] Discover Card   [   ] MasterCard   [   ] VISA
   [   ] Check or money order payable to Bonnet House Alliance

_____
Account Number   Expiration Date

_____
Signature

Photocopies will be accepted.